SEVEN
DEADLY
SINS

SEVEN
DEADLY
SINS

SETTLING THE ARGUMENT
BETWEEN BORN BAD AND DAMAGED GOOD

Corey Taylor

All rights reserved. No portion of this book may be reproduced, stored in a retrieval system, or transmitted, in any form or by any means, electronic, mechanical, photocopy, recording, or otherwise, without the written permission of the publisher.

Apartment 4 is a registered trademark of Houghton Mifflin Harcourt Publishing Company and is used with permission.

The Random House Group Limited supports The Forest Stewardship Council (FSC), the leading international forest-certification organisation. All our titles that are printed on Greenpeace-approved FSC-certified paper carry the FSC logo. Our paper procurement policy can be found at www.randomhouse.co.uk/environment

Printed and bound in Great Britain by Clays Ltd, St Ives plc

EBURY
PRESS

9 10 8

This edition published 2012
First published in 2011 by Ebury Press, an imprint of Ebury Publishing
A Random House Group company
First published in the USA by Da Capo Press, a member of the
Perseus Books Group, in 2011

The Random House Group Limited Reg. No. 954009

Addresses for companies within the Random House Group can be found at
www.randomhouse.co.uk

The Random House Group Limited supports The Forest Stewardship
Council® (FSC®), the leading international forest-certification organisation.
Our books carrying the FSC label are printed on FSC®-certified paper.
FSC is the only forest-certification scheme supported by the leading
environmental organisations, including Greenpeace. Our
paper procurement policy can be found at
www.randomhouse.co.uk/environment

Printed and bound in Great Britain by Clays Ltd, St Ives plc

ISBN 9780091938468

TO MY CHILDREN

whom I hope I inspire . . .

TO MY WIFE

whom I hope I endear . . .

AND TO MY GRANDMOTHER

who instilled in me the will to succeed.

I cannot call to mind a single instance where I have been irreverent, except toward the things which were sacred to other people.

—MARK TWAIN

Active Evil is better than Passive Good.

—WILLIAM BLAKE

Fuck it all and fuck it—no regrets . . .

—FROM "DAMAGE INC.," METALLICA

CONTENTS

chapter 1

In the Beginning— Or How I Learned to Love the Ceiling Fan

I always told myself I would write a book.

I knew one day I would sit myself down and pound words into submission—spinning yarns, webs, and tales of days gone by, of woebegone afternoons tinged with bittersweet delights. I would hunch above the paper and weave in and out of fancy, hoping I would be the next Hunter S. Thompson . . . or at least somebody like Anonymous. But I also made a solemn oath to myself that I would try to write something not only of value but also something that had never been done before. I wanted to do the unthinkable: Bring to the world a whole new subtext, a wholly different genre. I wanted revolution in wood pulp. I wanted death in the sentence. I wanted to reinvent the word.

Obviously this was not going to happen right away, and on some kind of masochistic level I was okay with that. I was still kicking emotional crabs out of my soul crotch, reaching for the razor while rinsing out the Rid. Anyone confused by that last metaphor can pat themselves on the back and walk away clean, so to speak. Anyone who has dated a stripper or lived with scumbags knows that scenario too well, and we have more than likely met at a survivors' meeting or two.

Anyway, between Tony Robbins and Dianetics, I really do not know what the hell is going on in the literary world today. People shill get-rich schemes on late-night TV disguised as tax dodges and government grant programs. "Celebrity" wannabes suck off traffic cops once or twice and are thrown book deals like fish to the porpoises at Sea World. When Paris Hilton can top the best-sellers' lists, we are one more Connect Four move closer to Armageddon. I wish I were being funny, but I am clearly not. No one this awesome gets incensed for no reason at all. No one in my zip code anyway.

I was hoping to have my shot at irreverence. I was hoping to be a shot in the arm for some kind of polysyllabic retaliation. Instead I am just hoping to keep from neutering the global book market. I mean, come on. What can I say that has never been said before? Between the Kennedys and the Royals, what could I possibly bring up that has never been uttered? Unless I plan on making up words, I might be lit out of shuck. Last time I checked, the written word has been around since those Celtic Hippies put little crazy tree symbols on anything flat and called it "Beowulf." So therein lies my conundrum: Much like Cialis, what will I do when the time is right?

✳   ✳

Fast forward years later, when I found myself across a dingy wooden table from a mysterious learned man in an exotic locale, seated for a meal of foodstuffs called "sushi" in a dark and cursed land known as Los Angeles. It was in this dinette of Japanese comestibles that I was toiling over this tome you hold in your hands, and I had reached a point of no return when this man posited writing about the Seven Deadly Sins. Now I countered that the only way to do this subject, one that has been driven into the ground with derisive frequency, was to give it my own unique and cantankerous spin. He offered that in order to do that, I should start at the beginning.

I thought for a second. Doing so would mean going in harder than I have ever allowed myself to do in the past. So I asked, "The very beginning?"

He said, "Hey, those are my spicy tuna rolls."

"Oh, sorry. I thought they were my B.C.S. rolls."

"Do they *look* like your B.C.S. rolls?"

"Well, if you squint and look at them from the side . . . "

"What the hell are you talking about?"

"Wait, what was the question again?"

I know what you are thinking. You are asking what that whole last exchange has to do with anything. Well, I will tell you the very key to this whole disaster lies in that little tête-à-tête. For starters, they were indeed his spicy tuna rolls and, by fuck, do not forget it. But more importantly, it gave me a launchpad, an academic Cape Canaveral to blow my little Sputnik into the hearts of a world that might not be ready for this Great Big Mouth.

From the beginning, huh? Insert long, dramatic sigh . . . and begin.

*   *

For me, it all started one frigid bastard of a night in 1995.

I was twenty-two years old, a hard-on with a pulse, wretched and vice-ridden . . . too much to burn and not enough minutes in an hour to do so. The year 1995 was a full 365-day year of drinking, fucking, lying, raging, and exploring. It was a time of *self*-shit: self-importance, self-absorption, self-indulgence, and selfishness. I was the only person in the known galaxy, and I wanted what the fuck I wanted sooner rather than later. The gift of life was horseshit; all I wanted was everything and I wanted it fast. There are certain mornings when I can still feel that year in my joints and the fatty tissue of my back. The crazy thing is that if I could do it all over again, I would, but this time I would take it even further than before.

I was a drifter with no leash, no money, and no cares. I slept wherever my body fell, sometimes because I was exhausted, other times because the people I had gone to "the party" with just left me in the middle of nowhere. The thing you have to remember about "nowhere" is it is merely a combination of "now" and "here." Grammatically I know that is incorrect, but if you have not spent your whole life in the Land of Nowhere, you do not know what the fuck you are talking about.

When you are stuck in an insurmountable situation, things like sin and hell do not really cross your radar or increase the pressure in your moral barometer. You do not give a shit about consequences as long as you get off and get off hard. You have an image, of course, but unless the Holy Ghost himself comes up and points a loaded .38 at your face and compels you to repent, there is a rat's ass chance in Hades that you would comply. These are the psychoses that fester when your world is a vacuum. Bring on oblivion, just do not change the fucking channel.

In 1995 I was an absolute crazy person. I caught gonorrhea twice. I took to "stage-diving" off of van roofs and onto strangers in parking lots. I picked fights with douche bags openly brandishing guns. I set myself on fire at parties. You see, this was not Bridge Club; this was hopeless abandon. This was *Mad Max* and *Gummo* all rolled into one. Get it done before you drown in a river of shit was our motto. It did not matter: Too many of my friends were dying or going to jail. Pretty soon there would not be anyone left to throw a party. So do what thou wilt with the soul provided. If I was going to burn, it was going to be on my terms.

Then one night in 1995, there was a party. I know that is a bit redundant because there was always a party. But this one was different. There was a stink like destiny on the smoke. There was legend around the corner. And for some reason, I was always in the middle of it. To this day, I could not find this house on GPS if you held a gun to my head. I could not tell you the owner's name if you paid me. But I remember the insides like it was yesterday. And it all started in the garage.

* *

I am getting ahead of myself. Let me set the scene.

Every weekend the unclean would descend on a little building in West Des Moines called Billy Joe's Pitcher Show, a tawdry little place that housed a karaoke bar, a concession area, four bathrooms, and the world's single greatest movie theater ever. No stadium seating like you see today—just '70s tables with '70s chairs and all the '70s ashtrays you could fill. During the week there was little fanfare—$1 movies reaching the end of their theatrical release and $2 Jell-O shots for caterwauling yuppies "singing" Huey Lewis covers. But on the weekends, this was ground zero. This was our turf because every weekend Billy Joe's Pitcher Show presented *The Rocky Horror Picture Show*.

From all over Iowa, tribes of misfits packed the place. The movie did not really matter, you see. There was nowhere else to go. You had to be twenty-one to get in a bar, and this was the era just prior to the great resurgence of all-age shows. There were no youth centers (well, no youth centers you'd want to go to, and some were dangerous), and no one was legally allowed to gather in parks after the curfew, which I never bothered to learn. To quote Henry Rollins, "your choice was fish." We were the greatest motherfuckers of our generation and we had nothing to do. So we turned nothing into something, mostly out of nothing at all. Billy Joe's became the rallying point. Billy Joe's became the catalyst. And we defended it with our own blood.

Call one of us a fag, and we all threw down. Call one of us a loser, and you'd be dealt with severely. Just because you did not understand us, it did not mean we were wrong. We were amazing because we wanted to be, and fuck you if you could not keep up. We felt like the latest and maybe last great iconoclastic surge, and it did not matter if the world did not know our names. The world was not allowed to join our club.

The party began at the theater, as always. We would pass the hat, buy as much shitty booze as possible, and eventually invade some house with a bit of room, a radio of some sort, and a lot of insurance. This night we managed to procure shelter from the storm in a three-bedroom, two-bathroom, two-story, cookie-cutter house in the suburban hell known as West Des Moines. That, as they say, is when the real fun began. In fact, to this day, people merely refer to the following series of events as The Night.

I have faint memories for the first few hours: shots of Jager, vomiting, jumping on moving cars, more shots of Jager, smoking on a couch when I was not even supposed to be smoking inside, even more shots of Jager . . . it is always the nights you cannot remember that eventually become the stories you don't forget. During a lull in the roar of the insanity, I made myself scarce to catch my breath.

I found myself in the garage, smoking a cigarette, freezing my ass off, and sitting on an unforgiving metal folding chair in the middle of a concrete void. I was coming around again, the proverbial second wind, which was usually when I ended up doing the most damage. The halo of liquor was giving way to the horns of ingenuity, and I was reveling in the moment, sober enough to appreciate it and drunk enough not to take notes. Later I learned that you have to live *in* those moments, not *for* them. If you look too hard, they blow right by you. If you do not live enough, you will regret every breath. So I was reflecting, but not too much. I was just getting started.

And as it turns out, at that exact moment, the starter pistol happened to walk through the garage door. For the sake of our story, we will call her "Beth." She was a fiery-eyed, raven-haired miscreant from parts unknown, prone to wearing black and fluttering her heavily shadowed eyelashes. She had a pheromone about her that just screamed "lust." And we had been flirting for weeks.

Beth slid slowly through the door and stopped at the top of the stairs leading into the garage. As I looked up, she said something low and seductive. Being smoother than chocolate pudding, I fired back, "Huh?"

"I said, 'whatcha doin', silly?'" Her eyes were burning with a cross between mischief and innovation. Something was on her mind, and God help me I wanted to know what it was.

She came and sat in my lap and kissed me slowly. It was then that she revealed her plans: I was to be the lucky winner of a threesome with her and another girl who we will call "Kelly," who was on the other side of the sexual spectrum but equally enchanting. As if on cue, Kelly came in the garage and sat on my lap as well. I have got to tell you, when two girls are straddling you like a pommel horse, you are subject to the will of your crotch. Lust is a lozenge I live to savor for days. But we will get back to that sooner than later.

So let's review: Our hero has just imbibed copious amounts of alcohol, thrown up, and has now been propositioned for a threesome with two comely vixens. Things could not look better, right? Well, as I have been shown time and time again, fate hates us all.

We sequestered ourselves to one of the bedrooms, most likely the host's parents' room based on the Spartan layout and garish décor. But it didn't matter what it looked like; the lights were soon off and pesky clothes shed in haste. Mouths found skin— those "sticky fumblings" that Hannibal Lecter described with such relish—and soon the three of us were a Chinese puzzle with no solution, a delicious triangle of heat and ferocity. The girls were giggling and moaning. I was happy for them to do what they wanted to each other, as I, too, was extremely busy.

As this was taking place, a coup was being plotted downstairs. A bum rush was about to happen, the definition of that phrase being "a large group of people invading a space they were not invited to, nor has enough room to handle their numbers." Forty people whispered and giggled, determined to inject themselves into our festivities, at just the right moment. It did not help matters that my best friend, Denny, was Cobra Commander behind this fiendish scheme, but it made sense because he was the guy I had appointed to watch the door so nobody would interrupt us.

Well, just as three bodies were learning new ways to occupy the same space (and just when it was getting very, very good), the door burst open, the lights flew on, and a multitude of cheers and jeers sounded the great chorus that officially put an end to our sweet little tryst. Needless to say, I was very angry, but seeing the good-natured mischief on everyone's faces, I slowly let that ebb from my mind and, climbing out of bed buck naked, proceeded to throw my soiled yet unfulfilled condom at the closest gawker.

As I was putting my clothes back on and watching the crowd gathered at the foot of the bed getting larger, I had a magnificent idea. Maybe it was the booze coursing through my blood stream. Maybe it was my eyes still recovering from the shock of the lights being turned on. Maybe it was because I just wanted to give these fuckers a taste of their own medicine. But I had the idea in my head, and no one was going to stop me from doing what I wanted to do. It was simple: I was going to stage dive off the bed onto the big pocket of onlookers, and they would crowd surf me out the door and down the stairs to the bar in the kitchen, where I would make myself a drink.

It bordered on ingenious. How could it not work? I was *Corey Fucking Taylor*, even then. So, pulling on my pants (I was at least that courteous), I leapt onto the bed and jumped . . . and flew head on into a ceiling fan that I had either forgotten was just above the bed or just did not see because of drunken tunnel vision. I swear to you, and this is not for comedic value or to belie any weakness on my part, this had to be the strongest ceiling fan known to humankind. I am talking industrial strength, folks. It hit me three times in the space of two seconds: once in the forehead, once right between my eyes, and the last bruised the tip of my nose. It gashed my head open and gave me two black eyes. I mean, one second I was the coolest dude at the concert, the next I was on my back trying to figure out what the fuck just happened. It was so fast that I did not even know it until I realized someone was helping me, in a daze, off the floor. And God love my friends, they never told me how fucked up my face was, so I mingled amongst them looking like Rocky Balboa until I caught my own reflection in a bathroom mirror an hour later. I should have just carried around a sign that said, "Take a Picture with the Party Zombie."

I tell you this story not to brag nor to build up some kind of false image of myself. It is just very important to this collection of insights and incites that you understand right out of the gate that when I talk about "sin," *I know what I am talking about.* This is no novice you are dealing with: Decades have not washed my hands clean yet. Think about this: In one night—hell, in one five-hour period—I experienced every single one of the so-called seven deadly sins. I was a mad-dog linebacker running the moral gamut of gluttony, greed, lust, sloth, wrath, envy, and vanity. And to this day, I recall this confounding chain of events with fondness and a knowing smile.

✱　✱

Which brings me to the reason behind this book, a reason I have embraced like a summer romance. I have cleared my schedule and my throat to call all of your attentions to a fading little fact that no one wants to admit because they are so mired in habit and weird guilt. I know you can handle the truth. I know you can take a shot to the brain groin. I believe in you, so believe me when I tell you this.

The seven deadly sins are *bullshit*.

Everybody still here? Anybody convert to Scientology because I let fly that little nugget of reality? No? Then we may continue.

For centuries, these so-called "weapons against morality" have been the big scary banners waved in the faces of millions. They have been used as the righteous fist packs by the Right or the Holy Brigade to keep masses of normally free-thinking, free-spirited folks under a multitude of firebrand thumbs. When the world seems to be jumping up and down and celebrating a little too much, fun-hating fuckfaces trot out these Golden Rules of Control to knock us all off of the Giddy Wagon. Why most of us cannot mind our own business I will never know, but I do know this: Nine times out of ten, sin is a matter of opinion, and in my opinion sins are only sins if you are hurting other people. *So* if you are not hurting anyone else, where is the damn sin?

Sure, the seven deadly sins can induce pain and malevolence in the best of us. They can overwhelm the greatest minds and the most stoic souls. But they can also empower and influence you to do incredible things at pivotal moments in your life. To say these things are mortal weapons that bend us all into the worst scum in humanity is an outright travesty. We all experience these feelings. We all struggle to maintain civility in a savage world. But there are times when it is our right as people to let these "sins" wash over us like a warm Caribbean wave. There are times when I say we, as a species, should just out and out revel in the sensations that these "sins" predicate. We are human fucking beings, for Christ's sake: We are not perfect. It is in our peculiarities where we find our character and individuality. Personally, I do not know if I could trust a person who does not have some grit left over from his or her past. We are defined by our dignity to rise above debasement; we are certainly better people for doing so.

They say "let he who is without sin cast the first stone." That is exactly my point. Not only are we all guilty of just being ourselves, we were never guilty in the first place. The only problem comes when we become caricatures of these deadly whims, like the politician who extols family values yet is forced to resign because of a dirty little fuckfest with a hooker in a truck stop bathroom, or the movie star who believes himself above the great unwashed just because his cheek bones are pronounced and angular. These people are *not* sinners: They are just shitty people.

I am not selling salvation here, but I am preaching moderation. Some of you motherfuckers are indeed crazy. I have no qualms on pointing out the obvious. So what if you like to fuck? Who cares if you enjoy actually having money, or love to eat, or are impassioned, or use your covetous nature to push yourself to new heights? Who gives a shit if all you want to do on your only day off is lay in bed and fucking sleep? Or if you think you are the sexiest prick on the planet?

Who cares? That is none of my business. It is *yours*. If you can live with it and you are not hurting anyone else, frankly I applaud you. At least you are not touting some doomed party line about the expressway to heaven. The whole reason for these supposed sins is really about control.

Think about this: A thousand years ago, the aristocracy wrapped themselves in so much excess that they should have burned here on Earth, but because they were royalty, they were considered ordained by God. There were no accusations of depravity leveled at them. In fact, the only time they were circumspect was when they killed one of their own. If they were given a theocratic pass just because of their birthright, what, in these modern times, makes it any more different for us? Sure, on one hand that sort of logic is a great reflection of medieval ignorance. And yet it would mark the very definition of America's founding principles: We are all equal. So one man's sin is another man's indulgence. Blue bloods glut themselves every day on the wants and needs of the upper crust. So when those of us in the middle or at the bottom do it, why should we burn in the house of the Christian boogeyman? Why should we be condemned for weekend indulgences that are just another Monday for the echelons of wealth?

So I say, "no more." Not now, not ever. I say covet the good life with every fiber. Cherish the spirits that make you feel flush and alive. Laze the days you are not devoted to keeping your family afloat financially. Get while you can, for tomorrow it may be against the law. Throw caution to the wind and free yourself of superstitious shackles. Believe if you want, but practice what you want. The days of fear are over and there is no turning back.

This book is a few parts flight, a handful of fancy, and a lot of why there is such a thing as freedom of the soul. We are vessels of profound depth when we have an inkling about why we are here. So why should we be saddled with inferred differences when we all feel the same? Just because we *think* something does not really make it a sin. Just because we *want* something, doing so does not make us sinful. Just because we *feel*, it does not make us sinners. There is real vitality in letting yourself indulge in what life has to offer. Quicken your spirit and you might just save your soul. Okay, maybe I am offering a hint of salvation after all.

There is, of course, also nothing wrong with depriving yourself of sins. But too many people put themselves on a pedestal for denying themselves simple things. Please, be pious on your own time: We're all alive in here.

Maybe with this book, you can figure some things out. Most likely, it will just help me work out some serious shit from my own life. I may be a fuck, but I am not an absolute fuck. Sure, I have done some things I am not proud of, but I would not call them sins—I would call them mistakes. You are not allowed to learn from sins because they are held against you for the rest of your life. That is, unless you are Catholic. Confession is like the fine print in an airtight contract, and I am sure most of the faithful envy you.

Mistakes? Well, hell, we all make mistakes. And what's more, we are expected to learn from them. It is part of our journey. It is how we move from innocence to resounding wisdom. It is how we keep from retaining a fucking baby's psyche well into our nineties. It is how everyone keeps from shitting themselves in public and on each other. It is our ever-learning, ever-adapting GPS for this thing called life.

Let me give you an example. At one of the several mundane jobs I held down before I became "The Artist Known as Corey Fucking Taylor," I had unbelievable access to all the resources and wealth that were held therein and took every opportunity to fleece the coffers by using my position and my knowledge of their security systems to do so. It was so easy to steal from this place that even the managers were doing it. So I joined in, not because I am inherently wanton but because I was fucking broke and I made less than jack shit. Now, I had not stolen anything in years. I had gone through my "shoplifting" phase when I was thirteen, and it was run-of-the-mill stuff like candy bars and Playboy magazines. So it was a novel sensation to skim tills, steal merchandise, and have sex in my place of business. To put it another way, I basically became the Caligula of the graveyard shift. I was a total scumbag: I stole more money in one night than I actually made in one week. I had orgies in the backrooms. And I walked away with thousands in retail products. But the real reason I did it was because I could. Is that a good reason? Not at all.

To this day, it makes me sick to think about it. It was a period in my life that I look back on in shame. It should not have mattered if everyone was doing it or if the people who owned the store might have deserved it because they were crooked as fuck, keeping hundreds of thousands of dollars off the books while paying us serfs like newsies. I have always been vehemently against theft, but there I was, robbing people blind and not giving a shit what the consequences were. I took advantage of a system I was entrusted to maintain, and I squandered it on avarice and greed. When it was over, I never stole another thing again. I do not take pride in that fact; I just know my boundaries and that is one I have vowed never to cross. But in retrospect, if I had not gone that far in the first place, who is to say I would feel that way now? If I had not done these things, who is to say I would be as indignant about it today? So the misguided acts of my past have brought me to the virtues of my present and will hopefully lead me to the grace of my future. But I do not consider them "sins." I consider them mistakes, capriciousness in the face of youthful abandon. I found my moral limit because I crossed my own line and did not feel good about it.

No one can hold me accountable. That is a job for my conscience and my soul. I am the only judge of what I am capable of, because who really knows me but me? Who really understands the road I have traveled if they can't even find it on a map? The difference between knowing yourself and trusting yourself is minute, but its repercussions are infinite. Now a lot of the devout will refute that by saying *He* knows you better than you know yourself. Yeah, that is great and all, but seeing as I have never seen any proof of his existence besides the nihilistic ramblings of billions of followers, I will take my chances with myself, thank you very much. Like I said, nobody knows me better than myself, and I learn from my mistakes.

Can you imagine how boring life would be without the seven little spices? You talk about sloth, but why would men and women get out of bed if there were no lust? Why would people want to be in a band if they couldn't feel the rush that rage brings to the musical table? Why would anyone want to be a bleeding heart without even a hint of greed in their dirty little soul? Why would the world go round if there weren't a few rules to break? A few revolutions to make? Let's put it this way: Why would you want to take a deep breath if you were expected to hold the damn thing?

Sure, I am making a case for the defendants, but then again most petty sins are simply excuses to buck the system and feel alive. Why have free will if you cannot put a few miles on it first?

It is like comparing felonies and misdemeanors: Stealing candy is not the same as murder, and lust does not always mean rape. It is important to remember these distinctions before we go any further. If you can't, you will never get my humor and you will always think I look fat in this skirt. Damn, there's my vanity coming out again.

Oh, who am I kidding? I could just be looking for any excuse to be a lecherous mook. That is half the fun, right? Remember when you were a kid and you would try any improbable excuse to get out of trouble? That could very much be the case here. I do not want to be saved; I just do not want to burn. I mean, I am a cynic, but I am not an idiot. I could be way off in my assumption that there are no pearly penthouses in the sky, no vengeful angels waiting to smack me around with their halos to shake the excess rust off of my bones. What do I know? I do know this: If there are loopholes in the laws this year or the next, I am jumping through with both boots because life is not supposed to be fucking dull. We are walking, talking, breathing reasons for beating the odds, and I do not believe after all of that we were meant to spend this miracle mastering the art of knitting. Unless, of course, you really like knitting.

I do know it does not take a sinner to sin. It does not take a Doubting Thomas to feel guilty. We are all cut from the same cloth and we all have bouts of insanity. But are these not just the rapturous whims of our enamored skins? I defy anyone, from Gandhi to Gallagher, to show me they are not susceptible to pleasure on any level, whether it is a chocolate bar or an orgy at a swingers' club. "Sin" is so ingrained into our culture that we are all capable, and culpable. Our very universe, when it is not expanding to make room for better, newer ideas, thrives on that which we cannot or should not have. So if you can afford the down payment, why should you not exploit it? If you still have the stamina, why should you not attain it?

The Haves and the Have-Nots have been doing bloody battle for aeons. The class system has been a part of our lives since the day we started washing our loincloths. Is that not a part of this whole thing as well? If you are a little better off, you can turn your nose up at the masses and say they are where they are because they didn't try hard enough, that the sin of the poor is sloth and envy because they long for what we have and are not willing to sacrifice for the bounty that life can provide. If you are on the other side of the tracks, you can ball your fists up and say that the bourgeoisie were handed their wealth, that they are sinners on every level—greed, gluttony, lust, vanity—across the board.

Morals and superstition have controlled the best of us for centuries. They have also allowed intelligent minds to give credit to deities that may or may not exist for human advances and victories for much longer than I have been alive. So the dark side of the lucky penny becomes the hidden agendas of the egocentric. Sure, you will cure cancer in the name of God's will, but if you want to be a decadent pig, you are on your own. Why should you not fuck for God? Why should you not attack a Vegas buffet for Jehovah? Double standards are too frequent, and no one is making a case for the defense.

Besides, where is the fun in being a zealot? Taking yourself too seriously gets you seriously fucked up. Zealots are the first to point fingers and the last to take responsibility. They will lead from the rear and survive by running away just so they can infect some other group who do not know any better. I want to be very clear: I have no idea what I am going to say next. My point is to make people think so they will not blindly agree with everything I say. The difference between a philosopher and a fanatic is about as thin as the profit margin at a casino, but at the end of the day it is very clear. A philosopher thinks out loud to make things better for everyone else. Fanatics make themselves louder because they think they are better than everyone else.

All I am saying is that there have to be choices. You live once, for all we know. You are given this gift of flesh and sentient thought, and you want to hole up in a cave your whole life? What about adventure? What about excitement? What about rewriting the rulebook to concur with a society that doesn't believe in fairy tales? The constitution of the United States is occasionally amended to reflect the mood of the people, but it is staunchly defended as well. So why not look at the facts, not the fables? The seven deadly sins—being greed, gluttony, lust, pride, wrath, envy, and sloth—should be changed to the *seven petty sins*. They are outdated and hardly deadly—barely PG-13 in this decade. What about murder? What about theft, embezzlement, and Ponzi schemes? You do not have to steal to be greedy, but you do not have to be greedy to steal. That may seem redundant, but take a second and think about it. It will make a sense too terrible to let go.

The time has come for a spiritual reshuffling, a kind of esoteric game of bingo. We can make a world based on common sense if we really wanted to, but we do not. That is a sin in and of itself: We have the intelligence and wherewithal to build a better mousetrap, but we are all very happy to run the game by the old rules. When punishment gets good to you, the time may be overdue to reevaluate the allegiance you place in your guides.

That's like ending up addicted to Ben Gay because you are used to being on your knees.

Make mine life. I would rather see people enjoying themselves than the few controlling the many. The status quo has always been to ignore and pray that things just naturally work out. I would rather see my generation realize its own potential than see it slowly warp itself in the design of the one that preceded it. Most would rather have you toe the party line than think outside the box. So much for self-sufficient concepts: Satisfaction should always come at a cost, but the payoff should manifest almost instantaneously.

But I have hope. And at the end of it all, that is what this book is all about. Hope that people can stop holding themselves back even slightly and start realizing potential they never dreamed existed. Hope that people can stop carrying the bricks of guilt and self-disgust and use them to build a foundation on their own morals, not someone else's expectations. The strong from the past always plant the seeds of the future. We have great reserves of good in us, and I have seen them firsthand. Ancient bylaws and tomfoolery have warped the way toward a life that makes more sense and less enemies. I want this book to make you decide whether or not your supposed sins are even worth holding onto rather than just using them as excuses to appear kind when someone important is watching.

This book is also about the fun you can have when you stop holding yourself back. It is a look at a life that could have gone horribly wrong, and yet with the right head on its tattooed shoulders, it took the right way toward a better way—know what I'm saying? I could have become something to despise. Instead, I found a way to be more than anyone expected, and I did

it on my terms. But I had some serious fun along the way because I never limited myself. Never. I live at the speed of my
mind, and I love with the strength of my heart. I am happier
than I have ever been. But only because I know where I have
been.

You can push the boundaries as far as you want if you know
where the state line is. We sometimes forget that time is on our
side—not blocking for the other team. I have nothing against
God, but it is not because I am a believer. It is mainly because I
have never met him, and based on his track record, I do not
need to.

If God does exist, and I am not saying he does, but if he does,
he is like a football team with a .500 record. Sometimes he gets
it right and sometimes he doesn't. I have to be honest: Even Ms.
Cleo had better stats than that and she had her own commercial.
Before you say "sure, he does," the fucking crystal cross one does
not count. Putting the Lord's Prayer inside it like some holy-
moley View Master is not cool; it is just plain creepy. Those are
the same people who sell you movable smokeless fireplaces
made by the Amish. Yeah, like we believe that con for a red-hot
minute.

This is the first step toward letting go of mythological rules
and grabbing onto one another, human being to fucking human
being, Hands Across America–style to reach the next damn step
in evolution. I say we should leave behind our tiny gods and
their baselines for "their" expectations. I say we drop our old
bags in the garbage and buy new shit at the airport. We should
be escaping the plastic pubis of the deities we create and seeking
new employ through a metaphysical Craig's List search. Stop
the presses: Earth just realized it could do what it wants. Let me

ask you: If you were God and you could have and do anything with just a thought, why would you hang onto this experimental ant farm any longer than it takes to turn your head to build another one? We are not puppets of papists. We are not extras in Jehovah's student fucking film. We are a race of people trying to find answers, and to me, religion is kind of like last year's textbooks: out of date with too many notes in the margins from the last fucking guy.

Maybe people will figure it out. Then again, maybe not. As much as it is in our nature to fight, it is also in our nature to follow the person in front of us. Honestly, that is not an admonishment. That is just us. We the people are we the willing, but there is just enough piss and vinegar in our souls to shuffle off the baggage of this mortal coil and get to enlightenment. And the seven deadly sins should be among the first to go.

So open up your minds and read on. Keep in mind the state of life and go forward. If I am prepared for the repercussions, then you should be prepared for my tiny little reprimands. It is your life, not theirs. Forget the buzzwords and the bullshit issues and *think* for your fucking selves. When the books open up, we should be throwing wrenches in the plot for better days and better ways. When that happens, we will be students again, ready to pass our tests with flying colors. My credo is treat everyone like it is their birthday, but handle them as if they could throw up on the cake at any moment. In the end, this is not an era for sitting on a fence. This is an era to tear that fucking fence down. Make your mark and find yourself; just do not forget to leave those cinder blocks called sins behind.

The great thing about believing is that the door goes both ways. You can do what you want. I just want you to want what has always been yours to have. The way is never shut if the light you seek is bright enough. If you are feeling a little dark, you can always change the bulb. Never let the limits of your understanding dictate how far you can go. We can be better.

We can just be. Trust me—it is as simple as that.

Wrath of the Con

Okay, before we go any further, let's just get something straight right now. I know I am opening myself up for bitter cross-examination here, but frankly I have had it. It is a simple fact. I know it and you know it. Deep down, in the same weird waiting room of your soul where we all agree Roseanne Barr was never funny, you know this to be true. Because nobody is willing to come out and say it, I will be the motherfucker and make it official.

Movie theater nachos are not real nachos.

They are not. Movie theater nachos are nothing more than chips and dip. First of all, you do not put your own nachos together, and you certainly do not put them together in a giant dark room with no table. Second, real nachos are more than just shitty tortilla triangles with a sealed Dixie cup full of spicy, runny Velveeta, and I don't care how long you microwave that tripe.

Real nachos are an event, a glorious commingling of meats, cheeses, peppers, chipotle, sour cream, guacamole, and crispy

25

maize saucers for two or more people bent on abdominal destruction. Nachos should be a mountainous conflagration, a majestic Tex-Mex experience in which every bite is delicious yet no two bites taste the same.

Movie theater nachos are a fucking lie. They are a public travesty to all things edible, a moral distraction brought on in an attempt to reshuffle a stagnant menu produced by an industry pigeonholed by their own narrow views of "snack time." It is not our fault their most popular items are the same three we have had for years—popcorn, soda pop, and candy. But they did it to themselves. If they had started out with a wider array of foodstuffs, we would not even be having this damn conversation. But I will *not* let my beloved nachos fall victim to this. I will fight with every breath to keep my nachos pure and disgustingly elaborate. Every breath, motherfuckers!

Good, now I am pissed, so it is the perfect time to talk about wrath.

You know the feeling. Darkness boxes your line of sight on either side. Your vision itself gets blurry; you can almost see demons in the trails your eyes trace across the room. There is bile that seems more like venom than saliva in the back of your mouth. Your fists clench and unclench until the palms of your hands tear open, and blood starts a sad journey to the ends of your fingers, mapping out the events that led to this debilitating state of mind. Psychologically, you can shift several ways. You can become loud and abrasive, abusing friends and family, cursing, regressing intellectually. You can also slip into a deadly silence, the calm before the storm, suffocating the world with the quiet known only before all hell breaks loose. One thing will always remain the same: As passion goes, wrath—or rage—is nearly indistinguishable from love in its intensity, the two epic ends of the maelstrom that makes us human.

Sure, it looks fancy. It is easy to wax poetic about this simple emotional mechanism. We all know the feeling too well. Some people cry; most scream their throats bloody. But it is truly the one "sin" on our list that unites us. Most of us can cope or subdue our lusts, our appetites, our lack of drive, our selfish sides, our tendencies to covet, and so on.

But we all get mad.

Admit it.

Just fucking admit it.

We all get mad.

Personally I do not see anything wrong with it.

To rage is to feel, just like love and hate. But those things are not a part of our so-called "Deadly Seven."

Am I right, folks?

There is a fine reason why rage is not a sin. When used for venting purposes, it can be so cathartic. It feels good to get shit off of your chest, even if it is someone else's turd stuck in the hairs. We gripe, yell, complain, vent, rant, rave, retort, and expunge because it feels really good to do so, and there is not a damn thing bad about it. It is a way for us to let out a breath, clear the air, and get back to what this species should be doing in the first place: dancing in the streets, happy to be alive.

However, wrath is also the one "sin" on the list whose darkness is immediately recognizable because it is a feeling that can be reciprocated instantly. In other words, rage is very contagious. All it takes is that little push, that little extra bit of selfish violation. It can pierce the very time in which you are witnessing and bring on a sadness that can linger for a lifetime.

Fortunately, a strong mind would blame the person, not the rage.

Unfortunately, I have seen the damage firsthand.

*   *

I was eleven when these experiences became a part of my life, and after this, innocence became very hard to come by. I had to grow up quick, and I did not do a very good job. It is amazing and sad what we have to do to survive sometimes. Every source of protection came crashing down when I saw the ugly side of humanity.

My sister and I were staying at the house of a "friend" of my mother's after a barbecue one night. We were only a few miles away from home. I believe everyone stayed because everyone we came there with was loaded and did not want to drive drunk to get home or so they could get high in the morning and catch a free one before having to crawl back to the "responsibilities" of real life. What a crock. There was no shielding me and my sister. For years we were exposed to every source of hate and anger possible. What happens to you when everything happens to you?

We were staying in the living room. I had one couch and my sister had the other. The house where we were staying was rented by some people I will refer to as Tom and Christine, mainly because I have worked very hard to forget their names. They were what I would call "professional adolescents" because they were in their thirties but still acted like they were sixteen. Watching delinquents play house is a lot like watching monkeys play poker: Just when it seems like they know what they're doing, they shit on other people.

Tom was out of work, but for all intents and purposes he was the most together of the two. He would actually hang out with the kids, make lunch, and take care of us. Christine was just a plain fucking drunken drug addict. She was a hole for men to fill up because she thought it meant they cared about her. She had three kids from three different guys, all of whom Tom took care of—kudos for that. She was a second-hand woman in third-hand clothing—obnoxious, loud, and ignorant. She did not give a shit about anything, and it certainly showed. How Tom could live with her I will never understand. But he did not live with her for long.

That night after the barbecue, Christine had bailed to go to another party. She did not even talk to anyone about it—just up and left her kids to go find more alcohol and bullshit. I believe my mom went with her because I do not remember where she slept that night. What I do remember is watching Tom get angrier and angrier as the hours went by and Christine still was not home. He put her kids to bed. She was still a no-show. He sat down to watch TV with me and my sister. Nothing. Sometime after that, we fell asleep on the couches. Tom passed out in the easy chair. Nobody had come home yet.

I woke up to the sound of someone pounding on the door, screaming loudly. Just as I curiously raised my head, it became very obvious that the pounding was in fact kicking. Someone was kicking the door in because the deadbolt was engaged.

It all happened in slow motion: Tom was jumping out of the recliner, the door was crashing open, and Christine was standing on the front steps with a forty-ounce Bud in her hand.

Then Tom punched her in the face.

Christine flew backward into the yard, too drunk to defend herself. She was yelling for help and calling Tom every name in the book at the same time. Tom heard nothing but the silence that had filled up the many hours she had been gone, leaving him with a house full of children who were not his own so these broken people could go fill their personal voids with the parties that should have ended in high school. All he could feel was his feet kicking her in the back. Then he was on top of her choking her. In the distance I heard an unfamiliar voice warning the two bloody lovers that they had called the cops, but Tom did not care—all he could feel was the pain of neglect, of being taken advantage of, of being a disposable afterthought in comparison to his wants and needs. All he could do was give in to the rage that was welling up and venting from him like a renegade steam engine, ready to blow if someone had not hit the pressure valve in time. He was a bomb with two fists, Vesuvius with a pulse. He wanted to destroy.

I watched it all, including the inevitable aftermath: Christine running away and Tom chasing after her, leaving all the kids by themselves. I sat up and waited with the younger ones. The cops showed up, hands on their guns. My sister started screaming, which set off the other kids. I told the police they had fled into the night and a few of them ran in the approximate direction. Sometime later, Tom was led back in handcuffs. Christine was screaming from the cop car. An officer was asking me for my phone number.

My mom's roommate's boyfriend came and picked us up and took us home. The sun was coming up. My sister was quiet for several days. We never saw those people again.

Rage is not a sin, but it can be the trigger that makes us commit sins. The real problem comes when we bottle up emotion and ignore the fact that we need to let ourselves be angry. Bad things happen when good people pretend nothing is wrong. I am sure Tom was a fairly decent person, just as I am certain that Christine cared about her kids. My judgments are based on the vague memories from an eleven-year-old's point of view. I remember the emotion more than the circumstances. But these things stuck with me because shit like that happened all the time. My sister and I were not protected from raw hate and powerful anger. It showed me that, with the right push, and the right pressure, anyone could be hurt at any time. That in turn made me angry, made me hate the world, made me distrust everyone. It was not fair; I should not have had to grow up like that. I turned it into music. Most people turn it into crime.

But then again, I still maintain that rage is not a sin. When properly expressed, anger can be beneficial. Some of the best art in the world is angry, jolting, and abrasive. Moderation—always practice moderation. You cannot place blame on the sin for one simple reason: If you blame one, you must blame all. If that is the case, then we are all guilty. The people who watched and did nothing are guilty. The ones who laughed and thought it was funny are guilty. The ones who suffered instead of saying something are guilty. Imagine a family tree of nothing more than the names of the people involved and you will get the idea.

The flip side to this rusty coin is that rage can make us do funny things. Have you ever been so mad you could not say anything? Have you ever been so mad that you just blurt out the most ludicrous shit known to man? It is a base idiocy that can be as infectious as the very anger itself. Try talking to someone when you are pissed off—words escape you and everything just gets louder and louder, to the point when you are using monosyllabic words and belting at the top of your lungs. You sound like an auctioneer with Tourette's syndrome.

To an outside observer, the telltale signs of someone getting angry can be hilarious as well. Their face might get red, then purple. They might start smiling or laughing while they shake their heads. Their lips might purse and their eyes will get all squinty like they are channeling Clint Eastwood or Steven Seagal. Watch their hands—they could either start squeezing or sweating, depending on their mentality. Teeth might actually grind if their mouths don't go slack from incredulous shock. All of these things are incredibly fucking funny to me, and I find myself giggling when people are incensed. That, in turn, exacerbates the situation. I cannot help it. It is awesome. Then again, it drives me nuts when people do it to me, and I become uncontrollable. I have to walk away to keep from firing off.

Sins are the unwashed marks on your spiritual record. So how is it something we all feel almost every day is counted against you? I get it—rage can send someone down a disturbing path that can contribute to actions of questionable purity. But getting pissed shouldn't mean getting burned. To be mad is to react to a moment beyond your control. Reacting to something you cannot control is life in a nutshell. How the fuck is that a sin?

Let me clue you in on a real sin; actually it is more like a shame, or a sad fact. Around the 1990s, it became all the rage to start *screaming* in heavy metal music. Nothing wrong there: I was one of the progenitors of that whole movement, and I screamed my dark little heart out every night. But then, something truly fucked happened. People started mistaking screaming for genuine emotion, rage became synonymous with all feelings, like all you had to do to appear passionate was scream in a metal band. "Oh he is so emotional . . . " Judas fucking Priest, are you *kidding* me? Jazz singers get on stage and bear their souls every night, and nobody gives a shit. Fuckbucket, the lead singer for the band Land Fill (with a logo that is completely illegible, illogical, and hackneyed, just like the music) barks the vocal equivalent of vomit into an SM57 with healthy doses of "fuck" and "dad" and people call him the next Jim Morrison.

It is not the emotion you are experiencing but the experience you are engaging. You cannot be defined by the feeling if no one knows what you are feeling, so it is the reaction that is the quote-unquote "sin." Why is the Church so scared of people feeling anything? I have a theory. I think it is because organized religion makes such an effort to control what people do that it makes sense to control how people feel, rage in particular because it is a natural reaction to anyone or anything controlling their lives. So how do you get people to stop getting mad when you tell them what to do and how to think? Tell them it's a sin. That is what's called a self-realizing philosophy. It is also virtually impenetrable the further you get away from the actual inception. In Martin Luther's day, you might have been able to reverse something so manipulative. Today, with hundreds of years of dogma and successful brainwashing under their belt, you can pound your fist against the walls of blind acceptance all you want. All you will end up with are bloody knuckles and modern frustration.

Yeah, if you could not tell, I have a big problem with religions. Organized religion has been the blueprint for more missteps than anything I have ever seen in my life. The thing I realized early on is that for an organization that preaches the benefits of love and calls anger a sin, they certainly breed a very opinionated and angry group of people, don't they? As I have said, hypocrisy is one of the biggest sins in the world. The effect of hypocrisy is that people are told to be one way, while the righteous can do what they please.

These people can sincerely go fuck themselves.

Much like lust, the only other "sin" that can be misconstrued as an emotion, there's a stigma attached to rage that has been dog piled by years of misrepresentation and fear. When a person gets mad, people are conditioned to think that person is immediately going to do something terrible. Some of this can be attributed to what they call "the caveman gene," but a lot of it comes down to propaganda. If I get angry, a majority of the people will automatically think I am going to kill someone or beat my kids or rape a horse or something else equally insipid. What is the bigger sin: the anger or the mudslinging about the anger?

Anger is a sin when parents beat their kids. The real sinner is the murderer who mangles a victim so badly she is left unrecognizable or the teacher who ignores the fact that he is supposed to actually teach because he allows his own negative feelings about children to get in the way or the wife who cheats on her husband because he did not buy her a big enough diamond for her birthday. The wheels on the bus may go 'round and 'round, but that bus might run you over if the driver gets fired.

There are so many levels to anger and so many ways to use it in noble ways. But rage carries the scars of centuries filled with unchecked degradation. Anger is a powerful weapon in the fight for humanity. Some would rather leave humanity alone, which begs the question: Which is the bigger sin, rage or fear? The adage goes "evil triumphs when good men doing nothing." Why would a good man do nothing to help the world? Is it a better thing to fear the unknown or to use righteous fire to fight it?

Here is an odd posit: What is bravery, really, but the potent combination of rage and fear? What is valor but being so angry and scared you do the unthinkable? You see, anger permeates society; when the niceties give way, we are all just one fight-or-flight away from eating each other. Can we get along with angry people? Of course we can—we do it every day. Can we get along without being angry? Absolutely not. It is not in our DNA to coexist peaceably. We can "play" nice, but we will never be fully cooled off enough. So how can we keep this in the "deadly sin" pile? Forget what the idealists and the hippies say; rage is here to stay.

This is fairly personal for me because I have always been angry. I think I gave up being cheery and gleeful when I was nine. As soon as my world turned upside down, it was over for me. So I suffered through poverty, humiliation, molestation, and abuse for most of my teens. And with every taunt, my anger grew. With every strike, my mind raced toward a judgment day that would have my aggression pouring through every street in every country all over the world. I wanted karma to drive stakes into the dark hearts that kept me bitter most of my adult life. I remember it all: I remember leaving school covered in food because all the bullies threw their trays at me. I remember memorizing all of the safe routes home because countless pricks with nothing better to do might jump me at any moment. I remember the prank calls and the toilet paper in my trees and the feeling that I would never ever be safe. I remember wanting to cry every morning before I left for school. I remember the shame and the bruises. I remember coming home to a house that wasn't safe either.

Now I remember all of their names.

I know what they do and what their lives are like: horrible holes of ignorance and banality morning noon and night. And because I am still angry—and always will be—I think of how those knuckle-dragging mouth breathers ended up.

And I smile.

I may never let go of my wrath, my anger, but I will *always* have the last laugh.

Is that bad? The Germans called that feeling *schadenfreude*, which means "pleasure derived from someone else's failure." Is it wrong to be ecstatic because the fucking bullies from my childhood turned into bigger pieces of shit than I ever could have imagined, and they are floundering in lives that I would not wipe my ass with?

I guess to some people, it would be. Do I think so? Fuck no. Is it a sin? Of course not.

It is damn near the definition of being human to be happy when your enemies eat a bigger helping of life's shit than your own portion. How else can we get through days that are quite clearly the "worst we have ever experienced"? There will always be a yardstick for our achievements, and it will never be tall enough. And we will always be angry about it.

But can we let go of the bitterness?

That is the terrible and guilty taste that anger leaves in your mouth when you have finally vented, and even though you may have felt the reciprocity, the bitterness lingers. You see I have been able to move on. I have been able to release, to tap the valve of hatred and turn it into something positive. But the bitterness circles around me like cigarette smoke. Maybe it will never go away. It is okay though—it takes a journey to know where you are.

Let's talk about something awesome, like mindless wish killing.

Now before you get all weird and beatnik on me, this is a harvested practice that has gone on for years. Everyone has angrily wished death on total strangers at least a hundred times in their lives. Think about it: the person driving in front of you who is either looking for an address or severely medicated. The people at the airport who have all the time in the world swerving languidly, interrupting the flow of pedestrian traffic. The morons who hold up the line at McDonald's, spending twenty-five minutes "ummmm"-ing for something that is on a menu older than most people reading this book until they inevitably order the same #2 with a Coke they always fucking order. Mall walkers, dog walkers, speed walkers, slow walkers—these people are so frustrating they make us all want to chew and ingest stained glass until we pass out from internal bleeding. Impatience can breed fatal fury, in which case we wish the most dastardly and fucked up demises on those eating up too much of our precious fucking time.

God knows I have.

And if you say you are too "mature" for that, you are either a liar or in denial. We have all "Jack the Ripper"-ed our way through a crowd of people before, albeit in our profound little imaginations. It is that "self" shit again, the attitude in which "the only one who exists today is me."

That is all fine and fancy, but take it from me: There is nothing worse than passive-aggressive anger. I am just as big a cynic as the next guy, but when a close friend's bitterness manifests itself in shitty smart-ass comments that knock the twinkle off of your twilight, then shit has got to stop. I am the first motherfucker in line to admit I have been extremely lucky in my life. I am fortunate to have a career, my family, even the opportunity to write this book. But when people I have known for decades come at me with this "remember where you came from" nonsense, it drives me straight up Homicidal Avenue. It is even worse when people openly refuse to recognize what you have achieved in life and instead treat you like you are still in second grade and it is your Friday to split the milk money.

Grab some pen and paper, children, here is another free lesson. The best friends you will ever have are the ones who do not make you feel like you owe them a damn thing. Some of my "friends" have a tendency to insert themselves in places they did not earn the right to be. What the fuck do you do there? If you call foul on the play, somehow you are the asshole, and that is five years in a small city. If you do not, it is your own damn fault and you wallow in it alone. See the conundrum? It is even better when your family tag teams you—thank you, Christmas. You are officially the worst thing ever. I blame Coca-Cola: god damn jolly old St. Lick My Staff, sitting in judgment on harmless fucking toddlers with their acolyte trolls—you can call them elves if you want, I know the truth—and it is the same shit every year. Wish in one hand, shit in the other: Do not get me wrong—I love ties like the next guy. But I draw the line at singing ties. Horse shit, whoever invented the singing tie should be lined up and beaten with every fucking singing piece of shit they are responsible for bringing into a world that did not ask for them. And do not even get me fucking started on Pete Rose. God damn Cincinnati Reds—I get it, one guy can make the Hall of Fame because he had huge hands, but ol' Petey makes a couple bets and he gets fucked. Do not even pretend that the other players are angelic.

Where in Truth or Consequences, New Mexico, did that come from?

Quite frankly, that just made me pee. But only just a little. It will be dry by the time I get up from my counter space where I am allowed to write in the kitchen, giving me time to have a cigarette, change, and be piss-free by the time my wife realizes I am in bed. That, my friends, is time management. It is also the story of Jesus. Really. Most people would save their mangers for last when it came to cleaning them, so the last place on earth people would look for the Mini-Him would be the garage, which is all a manger is really. A stable is just a garage for your horses and shit, or, more to the point, their shit. Managers will only rent those rooms if they are stacked for the night.

The thing about wrath is you have to know your buttons and who has got their grimy mitts on them. For instance, I hate driving in L.A. because I hit people. I do not mean hit them in their cars. I mean I hit their bodies with the car I happen to be driving. This is not my fault. The residents of Los Angeles plod across streets and around corners like they are (again) either looking for addresses or waiting to be touched by actual angels. You can blame the Pedestrian Right of Way Law in California. These fucking idiots just trot out into the middle of the goddamn street, so they are begging to be weeded out of the fucking gene pool. But because of this, I have officially hit forty-seven people in almost as many cars. Don't worry, I will not be arrested because as a rule I wear a fake moustache when I drive anywhere, in any city.

It seems California has cornered the market on buffoonery. Almost everyone there has a lifetime contract for retardation, so it is not my fault if they end up maimed or limping from a collision with a Chevy, know what I mean? Fuck them—any group of people that shiny, that handsome, and that stupid deserves a few wounds. It builds character; I only wish it made them a little fucking smarter.

You may be saying to yourself, "Does this guy even *like* other people?" That, my creepy unseen friends, is a great question. I have no doubts that somewhere in me I am actually quite fond of my galactic traveling pants brothers and sisters hitching a ride on this semicircular celestial body we call home. But for the most part, no, I do not like you. This is not my fault. It is *yours*. I do my best to get along. *You* keep fucking it up. And that, in turn, pisses me off. So do you know what that means? Very simple: If rage is a sin, then I am still not guilty because you guys make me inadvertently sin. You are all vicarious sin carriers, spreading godlessness like cooties. Rage gets the bolt of lightning because of *you*.

Nah, just fucking with you; thanks for buying my book.

*   *

Besides, I thought rage was a reaction. Rage is not really something you practice. It is a by-product of adverse stimuli. This changes the whole study. I mean, who should be blamed for something other people bring out of you? I think the people who elicit the response should bear the weight of the "sin," if there ever was a sin in the first place. Numbnut humans bring out the worst in each other and walk away scot-free. That is a fucking truckload of monkey shit. If you make someone feel mad, you get the sin. If you make someone feel greedy, you draw the technical foul on the court. This is just common sense. If you ask someone to kill someone and they get caught, you can still be charged right along with the other person. So what is the fucking difference?

The reason people are afraid of rage is the violence associated with it. Violence makes people nervous and nervous people cut up the land and stay on their own side. Like I said, everyone gets mad, but not everyone reacts the same way. Violence makes people hesitant to display their true feelings. Violence makes people flinch at loud noises on subways. Violence makes people think twice when dealing with—who else?—other people. It is the main reason we hold in our frustrations. It is why we waste time and money telling our worries to impartial therapists. Sometimes the stagnation of fury builds a conflagration of seething retaliation, bent on burning the churches and soiling the fields of our collective satisfaction. I know I sound like some kind of malevolent Nipsey Russell, but I watch the world without presumption, so I can safely say the rot of our reaction will always spoil the fruits of our creation. If you treat a situation a certain way, you will get a specific result.

＊　　＊

A long time ago I still had faith in people doing the right thing. Unfortunately, reality always intruded on this naïve notion. When I was nineteen, I landed my dream job of working in a music store. It was a chain outlet, but that didn't matter. It was the musical equivalent of working at Wendy's, but I was undeterred. I could listen to music all day and I got a sweet discount on all the CDs I wanted. It was a great gig even if I had to dress nicely, which I hated doing, but I did it with relish because for the first time, with the exception of actually playing music, I was good at something. It may seem stupid, but that made me feel normal, and even for me, normal is sorely needed once in a while.

There was one problem. I had long hair. That may sound extremely minimal considering today's standards and practices, but even as little as fifteen years ago, that was still a very big deal, particularly in the Midwest. I was not dying it, I did not have dreadlocks, it was not a crazy hairdo; I just had long hair. What was wrong with that, right? The answer to that question was "a lot," apparently. You see, in this chain outlet's regulations, it stated that a male employee's hair could not be past the collar. I could give three-fifths of a red shit about that, but I was not told that or made aware of that when I was hired. So a few months in, the owner showed up to do a walk-through to see how the store was doing. Without a clue, I introduced myself. He took one look at me, then without another glance he turned to his assistant and said, "He needs to cut his hair or he has to go." My manager did his best to defend me, but the damage was done. They fucking fired me.

Are you ready for the really fucked up part?

Across town, at another store of the same outlet, there was a guy with longer hair than me, and he had been working there for seven years. Seven fucking years. The manager at that store kept him hidden during inspections. I used him as an example for why I should be allowed to keep my job, but nobody wanted to rock the boat and say anything. I was fired; he kept his job until that chain outlet went out of business. I can only pray he is using his hair to mop out portalets in Toledo, Ohio.

So when the chips were down, people sold me out to save their jobs, as most people will. Even the other long-haired guy could have said something, but he did nothing. You might be asking me why after all this time I am still a little raw about it. In all honesty, I had not even thought about it until I started writing about it just now. So I guess I am still a little pissed about it. The reason I am pissed about it is because it was not fair and I am a firm believer in what is fair. If you lose fairly, then you roll with it and you learn what to do better the next time around. But being bent over and fucked like a freak so everyone else can fucking feel better about themselves for another few days is the very essence of why I am still angry about it. Yeah, it should not be that big of a deal seeing as I have achieved quite a bit over the years. Yeah, it was a temporary job at best and I learned a lot from swallowing my pride and accepting that people are still uncomfortable about men with long hair. But was it right?

I kicked ass at my job and I was responsible for boosting profits. I was good with the customers, and if I had been anybody else, I would have been in line for a promotion. I know, even back then I was not a big fan of compromise, and in the grand scheme of things it is a trivial matter. But what really should not have mattered was the length of my fucking hair. I was screwed twice, once by the owners and once by my friends. Do you still wonder why I remain mad about it? You give too many people access to your feelings and you will lose your grip on how to control them. For me it was a bitter lesson in loyalty and fairness. Thankfully people have come into my life to give me faith in those two precious qualities. But I still harbor lingering doubts about most people. I guess I always will.

My much larger point is there are going to be instances in life that make you mad. If anyone tells you otherwise, you should slap their hand because they just lied to you. So if that is just a fact of life, how can that possibly be called a sin? It is a given that you will be angry. The sanctimonious and religious will tell you it is another example of Original Sin and that God will be merciful if you ask his forgiveness. Are you fucking kidding? Who are you to tell me about "God," and if there is a "God" who the fuck are you to speak for him? Do you know God? Have you met God? Hey, here is an easier question: *Are you a fucking liar*? Have you ever had a notion that was not filtered through your God Ouija Board? Did God send you a text message from heaven? Did he use an emoticon with a halo? These holy rolling snake oil salesmen hold about as much water as a shot glass, but they know every way possible to quench the thirst of the bereft who are only looking for answers.

The darkest moments appear in the crevices we try to avoid. We traipse through events and encounters clinging desperately to the rope swing, afraid to let go. Meanwhile, the irony that is our essence seeps into those same cracks. The result is that some of our shit gets on each other. So are we soiled by our surroundings or surrounded by soil? What comes first: the friction or the fate? We can all drown in our dissatisfied mire for all I care. I hope the world gets Mono. I hope the world wakes up with its liver missing after a hooker dopes it—fucking serves it right for pissing me off.

But I empathize, you know? I get it. We have all got problems. We all have days when what we are eating might as well be dog food. We all have days when we feel like there is a sign above our mouths that says "piss here." Because of these peculiar days, we all have a tendency to shoot hot daggers through our eyes at each other. The souls of the world are crying out in anguish, and they are all saying the same thing: "fuck off and die."

The thing to remember is that you are not alone in any of this mess. We all go through the same things and we are all waiting for the steam to subside. If that means we are all sinners, then sinners listen up, pull up some floor, and cop a squat. Everybody get a little closer together. Do not be shy. Is everybody cozy? Cool. Check it: We all sin because they say we sin. So I say we stop listening. We tune them out like a local radio station. We should all feign a certain amount of deafness when it comes to the insanities of the clergy and the devout. But that could just be me. I happen to be a cynical son of a bitch. That scary bedtime story called the Bible is fine and all, but it is nothing more than a dusty tome for a dusty time. Never mind the fact that the Old Testament is just the Torah. Christians are so lacking in imagination that they borrow and steal for their own religion. They think they get away with it, but they are only lying to themselves. The devout Jewish look at Christians the same way Christians look at Mormons.

You want to know what pisses me off?

You all fucking piss me off.

You make me sick to my fucking stomach with the way you all try to fuck each other over. You bring out physical pain in me because we have been on this rock for approximately 200,000 years and you still cannot get your shit together. You are all sad, starving, exhausting, sorry lumps of aberrant cell reproduction, and I still cannot get over how much you all look like me. That in itself is enough to make me want to rip my own eyes out of their sockets and pass them around the glory holes of a porn shop, but the fact that you are all so satisfied, so fucking okay with all of this makes it unbearable. If you had more than two legs, you would climb walls. If you had more than two eyes, you would still have garbage on your breath.

So do you know what I do? I absorb all of this misused energy you cast around like semen at a frat party and I put it to use. I take all of your shit and all of your sweat and all of your fucking hate and I save it, so one day when you are all too busy doing to each other what you always do to each other, I will make you all fucking choke on it. I do not know how. I do not know when. If I could get the whole world to watch *Showgirls* for the rest of its life, I would not be as acidic toward it. But because that is not possible, I will wait. As far as I am concerned, we are not speaking right now, world. I know, I know—I will get over it, but not for a while. Not for a very long fucking time.

Do you know why I am angry?

You make me angry.

That makes me a sinner.

You make me a sinner.

Go fuck yourself.

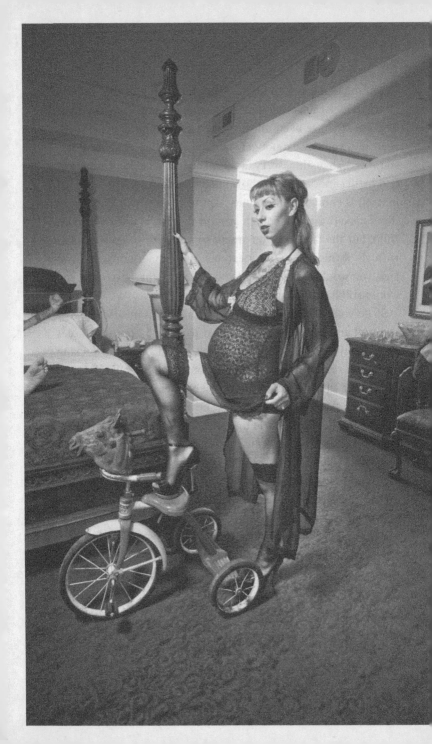

Lust Disease

I was in a beat-up bathtub backstage in 1999, and four women were preparing to piss on me simultaneously.

Welcome to the Lust chapter, kids.

Yeah, it really happened, and not because I am into water sports on any level. It was because when you mix women and booze, sometimes you just want to see how far you can go. We had just played Pittsburgh outdoors in October under a train bridge for some sawed off, shady-ass promoter. The backstage area was literally a pair of bored out trailers with a couch in one and an office desk in the other. So one trailer was reserved for our dressing room, and the other was sequestered to be the "after-show area."

After our freezing-cold show, we all washed ourselves down the best we could and commenced to carouse with the people. I never knew we had so many "friends" in Pennsylvania. A few too many drinks later and I had the idea for perhaps the single greatest sociological experiment ever lit upon in a Penn State shack. So, very confident and very inebriated, I climbed up on a chair and posed the question: "Hey!! How many girls want to piss on me?!"

Four hands raised in unison.

A mass exodus wandered into the cracked out bathroom. I stripped down modestly, reminding the spectators that it was cold and "shrinkage was expected," and laid my drunk ass in the tub. The four participants positioned themselves over me ass to back and, as if on cue, squatted. It was fucking hilarious. I laughed the entire time. That got everyone laughing. When they were done, I showered off and I was happy when they all joined me.

Needless to say, after this silly little spectacle, it quickly turned into a lot of sex, with limbs and mouths and fluids galore. Nothing is boring when you are ready to except the impossible as a possibility.

Lust, my Achilles Heel, the crazy monkey on my back, flailing and screaming and using my hair as a pair of handle bars, steering me toward the edge. It has taken me so far beyond the limit I could write a whole book about these exploits alone. It has also taken years to get it under control, to get it to the point where it does not make me do most of the stupid things that float through the Caligula-esque fantasy land that has been my life.

For instance, do you know the problem with threesomes? They are easy to start, but there is never enough room.

In 1995 I moved to Denver, Colorado, for a few months. It was a fairly big deal for my friends—I was moving there to get my music going because in my head, bigger city meant bigger musical gene pool and better opportunities. It was the only thing I was good at and the only thing I wanted to do with my life, so (ironically) I quit Stone Sour, packed my things into four big duffel bags, and prepared to blast off for the Mile High City. I already had a ride with my ex-girlfriend plotted and a line on four bands that needed a singer/songwriter ready for the big time.

But my friends were not about to send me off without a big fucking party. So the night before I left, we converged on a house on the east side of Des Moines and proceeded to drink ourselves silly. We had gallons of cheap-ass hooch and a house full of madness. Noxious ichors like Southern Comfort and Mad Dog 20/20 flew around in the face of common sense and good manners, so it slopped all over annexing walls and floors. There were only so many rooms available to hang out in, so a lot of us wound up hanging on the street, singing songs to the moon and making peace with the mutual pasts we might have in common. To them, I was never coming back. I was just glad to be with my friends one more night, and trust me, for once sex was the last thing on my mind.

Only two hours later, I was engaged in a threesome across the street in the parking lot of a church in the front seat of a Monte Carlo. I had one girl bent over on the floor of the passenger seat and another was leaned all the way back in the driver's seat, letting her holiest of holies get devoured by the girl I just so happened to be inside. It slowly became a complex pretzel of thrusting and sucking, juices and orgasms. I felt like I was being overwhelmed by smells and tastes until I realized it was the gas fumes. I was being poisoned in a wonderful ménage a trois and I was living for it. It was cramped as hell but it was one of the all-time hottest adventures I have ever found myself embroiled in.

If you could not tell, my life has quite frankly been one giant fuckfest.

One thing is for certain—I have never had trouble with women. And if I have one fatal flaw, it is that lust has always been the loudest angel on my shoulder. I lost my grip and my virginity when I was eleven years old to a very giving and fucked up babysitter, and it has been the line of iron sulfide in my stone cold resolve ever since. I came, I saw, I came again. What can I say? It is the strangest life ever, but it is the only one I have got, the only one I want, and the only one I will ever need.

It has made me have sex outdoors as many times as in. It has made me sleep with wives, girlfriends, and mothers of people I know. It has put me in situations in which being discovered by one's parents is less than wonderful. It has bent me to its salacious will for the better part of my thirty-six years. It is the Ripper stalking my sexual Whitechapel, slicing and dicing through my qualms and morals. And with the exception of a three-month bender five years ago, I have no regrets about it. Q.E.D.: no regrets, *no sin*.

Sure there are some things I wish I had never done. There are certain people I wish I had never seen naked, let alone done the hunka chunka with. There was a woman I slept with on my twenty-eighth birthday in Poughkeepsie, New York, that was misshapen, missing teeth, and wearing blue spandex pants I am still trying desperately to forget. Nature has a habit of letting some erratic genes get through. Fuck, where was I? Oh yeah, we all have a troll under a few burnt bridges, but what one might call bad decisions, I like to call whittling down my array of taste. In other words, when you are shelling beans, you throw away the ones that might get you sick. You feel me?

In our DNA, there is the built-in compulsion to breed, to procreate, spreading our "selves" as far as we can. The fact that it feels good is just an extra as far as I am concerned. Between the golden ratio and pheromones, it is a wonder more people are not fucking in the streets. So between instinct and free will, we get screwed, if you can excuse the pun. Man or woman, gay or straight, the intricacies of sex are major driving forces in our lives. Besides, a lot of our advancement is due to our wanting to get laid.

Think about it. How many monumental moments in history can be chalked up to just wanting to be noticed by some sexy peeps? Huh? Napoleon's victories, the Trojan Horse, rock 'n' roll, peanut butter M&Ms . . . well, that last one I cannot back up, but I am totally right on with the others. Men and women have spent generations preening like neophyte peacocks in order to press flesh, and yet along the way have managed to achieve so much. Who would have thought lust would carry us into the future? Makes you look at Star Trek a whole new way, huh? You think Bill Gates got any play without genius and a stake in Microsoft?

Here is a thought: Do you think Bill Gates can get an erection without crashing? Can he find a woman's V.J.J. only to have that sexual window close on him? If he gets pop-ups, how many viruses come with them?

Man, what the fuck am I talking about?

Who cares why we want to rub up on yummies? The fact is that we do, and calling it a sin is asinine at best. Why are people so ashamed of being human? Why do people attach terrible stigmas to instinctual behavior? You would think lust would be the one human drive that would almost be a guaranteed "Get Out Of Jail Free" card, seeing as any person with junk in their trunk and nothing good on cable likes to shoot sticky DNA on their carpet. Yes ladies, I know that is not how you work: Get in the bath, light some candles, and think about Gerard Butler then. God knows I do.

Lust gets the Scarlet Letter because lust begets dark compulsion when it is twisted by environmental agitation. Brutal upbringings,

disgusting mother figures, monstrous father figures, molestation—there is a heinous gamut of psychoses out there that can
wrench something that is supposed to give joy and turn it into
a deadly weapon. Murderers speak of bloodlust; no wonder
people get uncomfortable when they hear about real lust.

But here is the thing. People do not want to hear it, but this is
what I think. Everything I just described is not lust. These are
products or histories that lead to mental health issues. It is not
even close to the real thing, and here is why. Lust can only be
felt and released by strong minds. It is meant to be empowering
so people can embrace and enjoy it. Everything else is camou-
flage for puritanical denial. Nothing makes people feel guilty
more than tying implied darkness to sex and the inevitable lust.
However, if you do the math, rape is not about lust: It is about
hate, control, and sickening rage. Molestation is not about lust:
It is about generational abuse and a broken sense of self. Murder
is not about lust: It is one of the *real* sins I will address later.

Real lust is a celebration of the sexual self, a whole other side
of yourself that comes to life in the right circumstances. It is letting yourself go, trusting that the other person is there with you.
Real lust gets your blood going; it gets everything going, really.

In short, lust should always be accompanied by good fucking.

I know that is kind of crude of me to say, but man I have got
to tell you some of the best times in my life have been spent
naked and sweaty, not counting those times I was in a sauna in
Greece. For a very long time it was one giant Blake Edwards
movie, with excess and access abound. I can thank lust for in-
troducing me to the beauties of oral sex, both giving and receiving. Because of lust I am now in the know about a position
called the Hawaiian Monkey Fuck, which is a Tekken-like position that requires total concentration and the ability to be as

limber as a cat. It is daunting but extremely gratifying if you can keep from cramping—it is hard to keep your legs and back like that. So my advice is to stretch out prior to this endeavor.

Much like wrath, the shit that comes out of people's mouths when they are in the throes of lust is equally stupendous but in a hilarious sort of way. There is nothing like hearing, "I hate you! Fuck me!" I have heard things that have made me laugh so hard it has started fights midcoitus, resulting in departure and a case of blue balls. Women who fart when they are gripped by multiple orgasms, women who squirt when they cum . . . man, I cannot help it—when something is funny, I guffaw with the best of them.

That is not to say I have come out unscathed. I have scars that have their own little hellish tales. I have drunken visions of going to bed with one girl and waking up with another. They started out as the same girl, they just looked incredibly different, and better, in the dark. We have all had that experience of coming out of a whiskey-drenched slumber and all of a sudden your house is fucking haunted. And why do they always want to make you breakfast? I cast you out, unclean spirit! Where the hell is Max Von Sydow when you need him?

*   *

Instead of diving hip deep (no pun intended) into the usual suspects, I want to talk about something I find hysterical: the times when we feel anything *but* lustful and sexy. For instance, there is nothing less sensual than trying to look suave when you know you have to take a shit. I do not care who you are—you could be Brad Pitt or Rocco Siffredi—no one can find the stones to make a move when torpedo tube #1 is flooded and ready to launch, if you smell what I am shoveling. The turd pressure alone is enough to wilt the strongest boner right to the hilt. And if you are feeling unfresh, good luck with your game. This is more of a woman problem, really. Guys could smell like hot garbage and still be ready to go Casanova on the opposite sex. Women are a little more discriminating. Then again, women have much better taste.

That is really the issue, right? Men and women have very different triggers when it comes to lust. Most men are basically dowel rods in search of the next piece of wood for insertion. Women are multidimensional sexual beings; they are susceptible to attraction on so many dynamics that you never know what is going to float their boat—hopefully allowing you to put the motor to said boat. Where men only need a few seconds and a cocktail (again, no pun intended) to be ready for hot jungle sex, women usually need time, talk, and a good whiff of the intellectual pheromones. I know some women are just as chauvinistic as us dudes are, but I am merely making a point. Men and women handle lust in very different ways.

So here is my question: What the hell does "God" have against fucking?

We have just established that people do the sexy time in so many ways. If the clergy have the Holy Handbook, complete with merit badges, I would like to personally peruse the chapters and get a grip on the codex therein. Is it like a pie chart? Is there a graph with graduated states of arousal? Do the sins themselves graduate to misdemeanors or felonies? Are there subsections on certain sins in which the penance is more lenient, say for penalties regarding sex in public as opposed to sex with Myrtle the Cow? My final question is easy: If there is a secret manual, when do we ever get to see it? They leave us to our own devices to distinguish between sexual right and wrong with nothing more than recrimination. How does it feel to be left hanging with guesswork and assumption when it comes down to your immortal soul?

This is why I am calling Holy Horseshit. There is no book. There is no script. There is no Godly Guideline. There is nothing more than the personal opinion of those who are quite convinced that they are closer to God and, therefore, more important and smarter than we are. What an impossibly fucked up attitude. They stand on high and think they are infinitely better than we are. Well, the last time I checked none of my friends or family were guilty of child molestation. In fact, in my opinion, children are more in danger of being abused in a church than anywhere else. The Church cannot handle their own lustful ways, so how dare they question ours?

Again, do not get me wrong. I am talking about regular old-fashioned lust here. I am not making an argument for people who try to disguise or defend sex and abuse against children, rape, or anything else that is not between consenting adults. As far as I am concerned, there is no difference whatsoever between a repeat rapist and a NAMBLA member. That is not lust. It is a sickness. These people are nothing more than monsters among us, looking for another victim to terrorize in an effort to alleviate their own pain. They can talk all they want and hopefully choke on every word. My fight is with those who would take away pleasure that the majority of us love to experience.

And now, back to the faithful.

In terms of lust, of all the sins on the soul radar, it is the most physical of all of them. Sure one can say that wrath makes people want to take bricks to heads, but it is way more emotional in theory. Lust can be felt, but it is the episode one chooses to get involved in that really seals the deal. Religious folk will claim that even unfulfilled lust is a sin, but that is a copout designed to control how you think and feel. To me lust becomes "sin" in copulation. I may not be an expert, but I have definitely had sex. In healthy circumstances, sex is not a crime. So why is lust a sin?

I was living in Denver, enjoying the fruits of bachelorhood, when I found myself in what Papa would have called "a delicate situation." You see there were two women I was involved with. For anonymity's sake, and to make sure I do not get sued and lose the ten bucks I make on this book, we will call them Kate and Penny. They were both very different, very strong-willed women who I enjoyed many sweaty nights with. But I do not want to spoil the ending. Let me give you some background.

* *

I was one of several people living in a two-bedroom flat in Lakewood, Colorado, just outside of Denver off of Sixth Avenue. I was doing time at a video distribution company, loading reels or "pancakes" of blank film onto machines. The machines would then be programmed to fill empty videocassettes with the appropriate amount of blank tape so they could be mass-duplicated for distribution. That tells you how long ago this was—the heathens were still using VHS tapes. As you can imagine, with a job this innocuous, is it any wonder I tried to find any excuse or opportunity to let loose like a coyote on meth?

I spent a lot of nights out on the town, drinking my dirty little cares away and doing things that would make the Marquis de Sade look like Barney the Dinosaur. Word to the wise: Sex in a snowdrift is not at all worth it.

Anyway, I ran with a fun-loving bunch of lunatics, and these two girls were part of that group, fringe players in our little cabaret of chaos. Kate was from the South, a blond-haired, blue-eyed curvy vixen with a day job and night school who could turn any little phrase into something salacious with the slightest flick of her accent-tinged tongue. She was dirty, too; we had sex on more floors than we did in beds. I do not know how women deal with carpet burn sometimes. I am a wuss when it comes to chafing.

Penny, however, was a redhead through and through and the hottest nut job I have ever had the pleasure of bedding. Her eyes would light up before her anger got the best of her, so you knew instantly if you had pissed her off. Her body was delicious and her voice was a razorblade—it could cut across a crowded room at a party full of auctioneers. Sex at her place was a bit weird seeing as she slept on an air mattress next to an open window. Honestly, now that I think about it, I am fairly certain I only had sex in a bed like four times during my tenure in Denver. It was almost exclusively on the ground, floor, or the aforementioned snowdrift. Oh, and a handful of trysts in cars . . . goddamn those bucket seats.

I believe I was very upfront with both women regarding my intentions. As a bachelor (read: ass), I made it very clear I was not looking for a relationship. I was very much into being my own man, whatever the hell that means. To me, it meant "I really want to sleep with you but I will not be tied down." Now some men will lie about what they want. Others will be forthright in their sexual needs. I was the latter: I wanted fun and nothing more. Unfortunately, most women hear the truth and shoot it through the marriage prism. "Well, by saying he wants no relationship, what he means is he does not want one right now." Women, you have to stop doing that. If a man wants a relationship, he will more than likely tell you. If he does not, never sprinkle pixie dust

on his yearning and try to build a house out of clay. Take it for
what it is; it might change, but you are guaranteed to fail if you
push a man too far.

This is exactly what Kate and Penny both did. Pressure was coming from both sides, drinking and laughing was being interrupted
and serious dents were appearing on the high-performance ve-
hicle that was my sex life. I was starting to feel a lot like some
kind of gigolo ping-pong ball. And the sex was just *amazing*.
They were fucking me like they were trying to qualify for the
Olympics. I hate to say I was loving it, but holy hamster shit, I
was *totally* loving it. The gloves were off and we were all running for the finish line: win, place, or quit—it was about to get
weird.

At a birthday party, it finally did.

My friend, codename Mr. Nipples, was throwing a party for
his former girlfriend's birthday at their apartment. Booze was
flowing and everyone seemed to be having a wonderful time. I
was having a banner night, running from room to room joking
about this or that. But slowly and surely, darkness spread across
the festivities. I could not put my finger on it, but a presence
was lurking just off the scopes, a force that threatened to destroy
the merriment with zero remorse and zero mercy. At this point
in the movie, it would behoove the director to do a push-focus,
run the hallway of the apartment POV style, and present the
viewer with the shocking vision of Kate and Penny comparing
notes on their exploits with yours truly.

To me, it was not that big a deal. Neither one was my girlfriend. But as it turned out, they both considered themselves
"exclusive," the shadow cabinet to my prime minister. So right
at the peak of my sweet buzz, the two of them marched into the
bedroom I was holding court in and confronted me with their

grievances. I am fairly certain I did not make matters any better by applying reason and a nonplussed attitude to this fiery affair with the simple retort: " . . . and?" This set off a series of spectacular female assaults aimed at my person and my person's person that eventually led to me, stumbling drunkenly to my feet and muttering, "Well, I need a break. I am taking a walk." At least I hope that is what I said; at the time I could not really feel my mouth.

I wandered out into the kitchen, which was separated from the living room by a single 7x10 wall. Just around that wall was the front door to the establishment, which opened simultaneously to the kitchen and the front room. As I was heading toward sweet freedom, the birthday girl asked me in her own tipsy slur where I was going. Because I assumed it would not be a problem, I said for a walk to clear my head. For some reason she took this as the worst idea that had ever hit her eardrums and into her inebriated mind. So being a big girl and easily outweighing me by twenty pounds, she grabbed my arm to stop my hasty retreat. Not realizing her own strength and having no control at all because she was bombed, she half-pulled and half-threw me back into the kitchen. I was flung around like a rag doll, and because my own equilibrium was shot, I slipped, fell, and landed hard against the lower cupboards by the kitchen sink. My right elbow came down painfully on the '70s plastic or metal handle on one of the cupboards, and it pierced the skin, drawing blood, bone, and whatever the hell else makes up an arm.

With blood pouring down my forearm, the birthday girl tried desperately to rinse the wound, then, just as desperately, to convince me just to stick a Band-Aid on it. Luckily the commotion had raised the curiosity of the other partygoers, and I was hastily pushed out the door and into a waiting backseat to be whisked away to the nearest hospital. Because I was drunk, I could barely feel the pain even with my elbow bone sticking out. And unfortunately, because I was drunk, I passed out in the back seat of the car. I must have been on the verge of lighting a cigarette because when I came to, I had a broken Marlboro Red in my mouth.

I regained consciousness in the emergency room—face down, the broken smoke dangling from dry lips, and the sounds of Kate and Penny arguing over the top of my still body over who would get to keep me. However, the tables had turned: Now they were trying to foist me off on the other. "He is your mess—you can have him!" "I do not want anything to do with him, you can have him!" So as I lay there for another hour waiting for a doctor to come in, then another hour while the doctor sewed up my arm, the vocal equivalent of Federer and Nadal volleyed over my back the entire time I was in the hospital and continued the whole ride home, even as I searched all the twenty-four-hour grocery stores for a sling to put my arm in. I had twenty-one stitches in all. Because I could not use my arm, I lost my job. Because I lost my job, I ended up leaving Denver. Because I left Denver, I ended up putting Stone Sour back together, which led to my audition with Slipknot and other fine things. So fans around the world take note: If not for my lust and truthfulness, I would not have come to be the singer in Slipknot nor would I have been able to put Stone Sour back together, hence there would be no "Snuff" or "Through Glass."

And it was all because of my lust and a circular wound on my elbow. J. J. Abrams could have never come up with a storyline like this. The flames of lust do incredible things. They burn to the bone and heal into different skin configurations. They drive us out of our comfort zones and into the arms of destiny. They desolate our landscapes and show us the complexities of relationships. They also convince us to make out with an old guitar player on New Year's Eve when we are so trashed we did not know who was in front of us. I tell you one thing: That guy has a giant tongue. It made me puke. True story.

So I guess most of my adult life has been a road map on the in and out highway. If I am guilty of a deadly sin—and you know me, I am not saying I am or am not—my sin would be lust. But does it stand to reason that if lust were a true sin then it should have never been made to feel so damn good? Why is sex our fleshlike version of chocolate? Why do we get caught in the nets when they feel like heaven and taste even better? In other words, what the fuck, man?

I still maintain that it comes down to how comfortable people are with their own sexuality. The status quo has gone to great lengths to make sure the taboo is in the tablet. I mean, up until the 1960s homosexuality was regarded as a fucking mental illness. Is that a big enough control issue for you? "Those in favor" chose to make people who were confused enough as it was feel like they were fucking crazy. Can you imagine having to go through shock therapy all because you wanted to sleep with whomever you were attracted to? It is so hard for the gay and lesbian community to trust us; we had to go and try and fuck with their minds, so I do not blame them in the slightest.

Anyone who feels that homosexuality is not only a sin but also a disease or a mental issue should take a look in the mirror and realize who the real crazy person is. Of all the gay and lesbian people I have ever known, there has only been one crazy candidate, and believe me he was truly crazy. He was convinced he had wings under his skin. Now I am not one to judge, but that shit is fucking crazy to me. But he was crazy because he thought he was some kind of Thanagarian warrior, not because he knew who he was attracted to. There is a subtext to judgment that is hypocritical and openly selfish. If people spent more time minding their own business and less time in other people's business the world would be having a much bigger party. These are the same people who believe gay marriage isn't a constitutionally protected right. I bet the houses of their unions have more skeletons in their closets than brooms.

My blood is starting to boil, but I should be careful. This is not the wrath chapter. It is all things lust, all the time on this Sirius channel. Lust is such a fun thing too—it is a real shame that people cannot just relish it for what it is. Lust is a doorway to the very heart of our heart. Lust and sex were celebrated by many cultures as the tapping we hear on the doors of our ids. Mating rituals have been a part of us since we clubbed our first cavewoman. There are nuances and delicacies that we can still learn from our inner pervert. When we turn a blind eye and numb pelvis toward our spiritual horizons, we never get to see our suns peak. That is a mother-fucking shame.

Rest assured that nothing will be accomplished in the War of the Loins. Even if they were to legislate monogamous missionary sex by penalty of law, we as free-thinking rebellious folk would find a way to get around it. Lawmakers and judicious churchies, or Christos as I am fond of calling the uber-religious, will do their damnedest to stick their heads into our unanimous asses to see where our shit has been. But we—the few, the proud, the horny—will beat them back with the speed of our wits and the strength of our sexual resolve. This is not only the freedom we should all have but also the right we should all enjoy. The good fight starts when the bad shit happens. So bring it on—the world is waiting.

*   *

One brutal by-product comes from hetero lust though, and it involves panic, hysterics, and peeing on blue sticks. That is absolutely correct, Harry, I am talking about babies. For those of you not in the know, babies are tiny humans who cannot feed themselves, change their own diapers, or drive themselves to the gas station. For those of you (like myself) who are all too familiar with the concept of young ones, we are very aware that babies are loud, insane creatures who barely walk and never talk but cry continuously until they are distracted. Coming as that does from a father, please make no mistake, I love my children.

But holy shit, they will drive you to drink more.

This goes hand in hand with lust in general. The Good Book—and by that I mean *The Joy of Sex*—tells us "go forth and procreate." So lust is the lube for our child-bearing gears, the gas in our engines so to speak. It is a part of our genetic unconscious to spread our seeds across the lust-filled landscape, a postcard of fleshy reminders that we were here. Orgasms are affectionately along for the wonderful ride. Thank god for that: If all we got out of sex were children and migraines, humanity would have phased out genitalia centuries ago, along with pinky toes and that snot tunnel that takes phlegm from your nose directly into your mouth. I will never understand that piece of our anatomy.

When did the necessary get lumped in with the ne'er do wells of our sinful never can tells? Who put the Sodom in Gomorra? Were our ancestors so fucked up that they crossed lines even ignorant, undeveloped ancient fuckers found distasteful? I mean, did ye old lust lead to sticking your cock into mountains? Were people chasing down frogs? Was mud being plunged into

with romantic fervor? These are the things the Bible conspicuously leaves out. I bet you a handful of Chili's coupons that Jesus
had a foot fetish. People are just inherently weird, man. I got to
be honest; I have sucked my fair share of toes myself, and it is
some of the sexiest shit on the planet. Damn, I might have to
take a break and work something out if you get my drift.

That reminds me: I do not know what the Catholics have
against masturbation, but if there were a way to levee complaints on their heads, I would do so in an instant. What the
Catholics and Christians call a sin against oneself, the great
Woody Allen called "sex with the one you love." Masturbation
and a rented movie beat dinner and shitty conversation with a
bad blind date any fucking day of the week. Quote me on that.
A little push, a little pull, and a lot of imagination can be just
what the doctor ordered after a hard day. Let's face it, sex sometimes requires talking. For guys, sometimes quite frankly we just
need to tap the sexual valve. Pull up cam whores or your porn
or red tube or porn hub or a plethora of other worldly Web sites
that offer "visual horizontal recreation," then get a "handle" on
yourself and fall asleep watching *Forensic Files.* Besides, I would
never listen to people who spend too much time in wooden
booths listening to people's secrets all day.

The days of feeling humiliated about normal sexual escapades
should all be behind us. Sadly, there are many among us who
still equate sex with hateful things like rape and molestation.
Small people have small minds cluttered with smaller ideas, and
it is a shame that so many of them have giant reaches into huge
pockets. If I would never hand control of my sexy bits to a falcon
with epilepsy, then why would I be expected to do so with
strangers who have no clue about pleasure? I feel like I am going

fucking nuts here. And when I go fucking nuts, I have a tendency to break my lucky Guinness glasses. Damn it guys, I only have so many of those things left!

Sentient beings with intelligence and morals should be allowed to put their pieces in whatever Reese's they want, whether they are gay or straight. The stigmas of the past should be eradicated. The powers that be should be the powers of free. Brothers and sisters, the twilight of our sexual revolution is going to give way to the dawn of our lusty victories. We can lead a march through the streets of every major city of the greatest country in the world and proclaim that our privates are private property. No one gets away with murdering our right to coitus. No one gets away with controlling how we feel about how we feel. The right to bare asses is right up there with licking apple pie off the tits of someone called Big Mama. America puts the cunt in country, damnit. We are fucking alive in here.

I am a big fan of pizza, with ranch dressing handy for dipping. I had no other reason for writing this than to lighten the mood a bit before I pull your panties off. Do you feel me, earth? Yeah, that is my hand on your thigh and my lips on your ear. Besides, does anyone really like having a tongue in their ear? It is akin to a worm trying to take over your head. It is just gross. I would rather have a raccoon's dick shoved into my navel than have a tongue stuffed into either one of my ears. Now nibbling is a different story. Just give me some tiny bites on any part of me and I am rendered harder than mahogany in the Arctic Circle. I think I am going to drag my wife upstairs and rub something against her. No, I mean it. She has lint on her sweater and the sticky lint brush is on the counter in our bathroom. What did you think I was talking about? You guys are fucking perverts,

man—get your head out of the gutter. That is my wife you are
thinking about!

God, my wife is hot.

*   *

I have had sex with porn stars and rock stars. I have had sex with
friends and strangers, with beauty queens and the stuff of wet
dreams. I have fucked whores and hags. I have done so much
that it is damn near impossible to put a finger on just where my
own unique kink comes from sometimes. But one thing is for
certain: If it were not for lust, half my stories would be boring
wastes of breath. If it were not for lust, my little soirees would
be nothing more than campfire sonnets designed to lull you to
sleep—maybe not all of them, but most of these stories would
be anyway. For the last thirty-five years, lust has been my co-
pilot, I have been its captain, and we have gone down in the shit
together.

I do not think I am unraveling the mysteries or the science
behind our sexual drives or weakness. I am just a guy trying to
make you feel better about having sex in the first place. The
stains of the past can wash off with enough time and effort.
People, the power is truly in our hands. From soup to nuts, from
hello to the afterglow, from dinner to the postcoitus cigarette—
every decision, every move you make, and every vibe you gauge
is free will burning. You can dodge the bullet at any moment or
bury it with the closest bone. Although sex feels great when it
is dirty, it should never feel evil or, for that matter, deadly. We
all live with lust in our hearts, the passionate pulse of being alive,
and nothing the authorities say will do anything to make us become eunuchs.

So for all you uptight vanilla hard-on motherfuckers who are just hanging around the sandbox waiting for the first opportunity to kick dirt in our beds, how about you go ahead and stick your head deep in that very sand. The world is a little bit easier to cope with after a good bout of "Who Tied Me Up?," and I for one can keep from plotting the deaths of my enemies when I have had a strong six-second orgasm. I am begging those of you who just do not get it or, more appropriately, do not get it enough to lay off! Better yet, get laid and get off. If you could view the world through blue-lined glasses, you would see most of us are just having fun, just kicking the mud off of our bodies and spirits. It is a fucking jungle out there, man. But thank Pete we all came equipped with a great stress-killing mechanism that hopefully never disappoints, never dies down, never gets old, and never ever makes anyone say "ow!" Is lust a sin? In my professional opinion, lust is not a sin at all. But I will say this: Sometimes it feels even better when you pretend it is one.

chapter 4

Bonfire for Vanity

For those of you not very familiar with me, let me introduce myself.

My name is Corey Taylor. I was more or less born and raised in Des Moines, Iowa, although I had lived in twenty-five different states before I'd reached puberty. I am (apparently) a renowned artist, singer, songwriter, lyricist, entertainer, dancer (total lie), magi (another lie), aura reader (where's he going with this?), and all-around famous person. I have two very successful bands, Slipknot and Stone Sour, with multiplatinum albums and award-winning music. I have seen a million faces, and I've rocked several hundred of them. And I have been nominated for ten Grammies, winning one, making me the Susan Lucci of rock and roll. I also have had the privilege of writing my own monthly column for a British publication called *Rock Sound* since 2001.

Besides all those other super-cool things, I am a loving husband and father of two ultra-cool children. I am a manic geek who enjoys all things geek-tastic, such as comic books, movies, collectible action figures, and so on. I have been writing since I was nine years old, my first published piece being "The Tiger," which was featured on the front page of the *Jackson Journal* (to be fair, the *Jackson Journal* was the leaflet handed out at my old elementary school, and it was only two pages—but I did score the front). I am not Elmer Fudd and I do not have a mansion and a yacht, but I have three houses, a commercial building, and I hope to have a house boat by the time I am old, or at least young enough to swim after it when it gets away from me.

One more thing: I do not mean to brag or anything, but, goddamn, I am pretty.

Not just like Ewan McGregor or Jude Law pretty, but like Kate Beckinsale pretty. I know, I know, in front of a mirror it is all well and good, you got to deal with shadows and shit, but standing still, I cut a very handsome figure. Also, to quote Ani Difranco, "I have the kind of beauty that moves."

I have a visage so stunning I make women and men pregnant. When I move through a room, I leave trails of vapor that intoxicate even the sternest critics. My eyes melt butter, iron, graham crackers, and Silly Putty. I dance like Stevie Wonder and I blush like Betty Boop. I am just all-around kick-fuckin'-ass.

God, if only any of that shit were true.

I have just given you a taste of Vanity, this chapter's delicious little deadly sin. Self-love, the only true love, besides the love of food. Everybody has a little of it. It is different from pride: Pride is love for one's deeds or achievements. Vanity is love for one's . . . one, I guess. From vanity plates to *Vanity Fair*, it seems commonplace. It is very easy to explain: Most of us are who we are, but vain fuckers are who they love, and they will do whatever they have to do in order to ensure that everyone around them loves them, too. This is the grotesque by a whole new name; it is pure peacock syndrome.

Again, by and large I have no trust in the field. People who come off as very vain are pompous asses, and people who do their very best not to care how they look or act come off as—you guessed it—pompous asses. But if we're honest, we are all at least a little bit vain. We all have a need to love ourselves, or at least one thing about ourselves. But there is nothing wrong with a touch of self-assurance. That kind of empowered feeling can be the fuel for great accomplishments. But too much and you run the risk of having way too much in common with Paris Hilton. It's okay, you can think what you want about her while reading my book. There is no chance in hell she would read this because there are no pictures of cartoon dogs to color with magic markers in here.

Vanity is constantly checking every mirror, storefront window, tea kettle, microwave door, windshield and any other reflective surface just to get a glimpse of your fine self. Vanity is leaving a child's birthday party because one of the seven-year olds has a better vintage Van Halen T-shirt than you do. Vanity is pumping fat from your ass into the lean bits of your face and pretending people do not totally think you look like a flying coconut raped your face. Do not kid yourself, true believers (love you, Stan!): Vanity can be a dark, dangerous, hulking bipolar bitch that can chase you till the day you die.

But that does not make it a fucking sin.

Sure, it is ironically ugly. It is disgusting to see someone so into his or herself that your skin crawls just standing near them, with little more to go on but their constant use of "I," "me," or "my." But as satanic as it gets, the frustrating part comes when these people do not even recognize the issue. They think they are being confident—and to other vainglorious fucks, I am sure they are. But it is all in the details. They are trying to look like they are not trying at all. I can tell; maybe even you can tell.

A vain person cannot allow a conversation to happen without dishing in his or her own exploits. No matter what, it always has to be about *them*. Bring up football, they will turn it into a dissertation on how they were the best flag football player in second grade: "Could have gone pro, if there was an official league, but my friends are petitioning the state legislature." I really heard someone say this, swear to Buddha.

A vain person will size up the room to draw the most energy to his or herself. They do it by talking loudly, gesturing like a Shakespearian actor and laughing like a hyena on Meth. Mick fucking Jagger could walk into a smoking lounge in St. Louis, Missouri, on a layover to Africa in the hopes of raising money for impoverished natives. A vain person would still walk up to him and explain what he is doing wrong with his band. An expert is nothing more than a vain person who has read a book.

The deception of vanity is that it is not only skin deep. It is a soul-sucking disease that warps within and without. It makes truly beautiful people look like they should live under a bypass somewhere, bothering goats and silly knights. It puts the "shun" in pretension. The truth is that most people do not give a shit when you get down to it. Most people do not try to match their catgut belt to every thermos they use to carry their coffee. Most people do not roam around preening like an idiot. Life is not a fucking movie, and you do not always have to look good for your close-up. The emperor's new clothes are now a chain outlet fooling morons into thinking there is more to being less. We want our heroes to look cool, but they do not have to look like they are trying so fucking hard.

I have probably the worst self-image on the planet. It is like when I look in a mirror, the damn thing is warped. I have never been able to look at myself without picking out a smorgasbord of flaws and ripping myself apart. They could vote me one of *People* magazine's Fifty Sexiest Men Alive and I would freak out because I would be certain someone was setting me up to be *Punk'd*. I have days that are better than others, but for the most part I am paralyzed with a self-image problem. When you grow up with denigrating bastards your whole life, the feeling that you are filthy never really goes away. Thank god you can eventually align yourself with people who will do their very best to reverse this horrible predicament.

Back to vanity: Is there anything more hilarious than watching the mannerisms of a truly vainglorious person when they do not think we are watching? Their faces appear both pinched and glowing depending on the circumstance. It is like on one hand they do not want to be bothered by peons and curmudgeons who could possibly diminish their shine, but on the other hand they need these living mirrors to reflect their dazzle. They need us because without us they would never feel their beauty. Janice Dickinson looks like she should be numb because anyone that pulled on and stretched out cannot feel pain like we mortals do. Vain people do not feel it because they feel nothing.

But the question remains: Is this a sin? No. Being a preening douche bag is a *character flaw*, not a sin. So where the hell did this notion of sin come from? Something tells me a long time ago, there was one flake that just had to brag to the hierarchy about the gold-leaf tunic his mother made for him and he was so braggadocious that they took a vote in Ye Olden Temple to quash any further use of glamour or self-flattery. That is how Superman saved Christmas . . . oh, and that is also how vanity became a sin. This is also why religious folk dress like fucking paupers. God forbid they wear some shit that does not look like it was sewn out of carpet and fish paper in the 1600s. But people are so terrified of appearing vain that they will rob from the kitsch and live like the Amish.

Do not get me wrong, there is a difference between wanting to look attractive and treating everyone like beef tripe if they refuse to view you as anything other than spectacular. The gall of the truly vain is the supposition that anyone who stands fast to good old-fashioned good taste will be shunned into obscurity. Nowhere is this state of mind and play more prevalent than that breaker of wills, that fucker of hopes, that dreadful hatch full of fuck and cancerous rancor called high school. It is so true that even at the age of thirty-six, I can still feel like retching when I think of my tenure from ninth to whatever fucking grade I was in when they "asked me to leave," a nice way of saying, "You are expelled; do not come back."

High school is meant to be socialism for beginners. Instead, it becomes a strange TV movie for the feudal system. You end up with a commingling of everything bad in the world. If you are one of the Pretty Faces or Alpha Males, you breeze through those four years with little difficulty, signing yearbooks and cheating on tests with just a touch of date rape on the side for good measure. High school is a breeding ground for moronic creamy dreamboats who peak in their teens, for troglodytes who think life only exists from freshman to senior. Can you imagine their chagrin when they realize that if they are lucky they get eighty more years of life? That is, if they can actually count to eighty.

I got my fill of vanity from those limber years of shucking and running, fucking and cunning, and I have to say the only thing I take away from them are my need to put as many years between me and the wet end of puberty as possible. Those could be the worst kids ever, and they were being encouraged to become the worst adults ever. Are we living in a goddamn vacuum? Are we devolving like Devo predicted thirty years ago? A thousand years from now, will any of this matter? A million years from now, will we merely be the hottest, cutest dipshit boobs left who did not choke on their own air?

Pretty people come with pretty problems. This concept is very funny to me. "Should I use the mauve eye shadow or the burnt sienna?" "Should I wear my expensive ripped jeans or my *really* expensive ripped jeans?" "Do I eat at a place where I usually go so people will see me or eat at a place where I have never been before so people will have to *find* me to see me?" Are they fucking kidding me? These are serious questions? I cannot tell you how many times I have had to listen to some of these fucking Californians; they talk the most amazing shit because their heads are so far up their own asses that they can taste every fart before it passes their mustaches. It is a terrible, visceral, and violent mindset that twists and bends people like ancient oaks in a Carpathian forest.

But is it a sin? Or is it just another distraction on the way to death?

Neither is the honest answer. It is too boring to be a sin. Let me take that back; it is only a sin to yourself and is there a worse thing we can do to ourselves than sin? I do not think so. But a sin in general? No fucking way, dude. Vanity is too base to be a sin. Do you know how easy it is to be into yourself? Do you know how easy it is to ostracize your fellow humans because you are too busy shouting, "Dig me!"? Sometimes I think people are too fucking stupid to be this dumb. It is also too strong to be a mere distraction. I have seen it twist too many people in its wind. No, vanity is something else.

How that makes sense at all is a mystery to me. But as long as I get it, who fucking cares?

Animal activists throw blood or paint on people wearing fur and leather. I think people opposed to vainglorious bastards should throw Avon on them and not the high-end stuff. I am talking about the little bullet-sized lipsticks with the viscosity of rancid duck puss. Vain people are flesh mosaics of abandon and lack of confidence. They are terrified of appearing anything other than perfect. What a sweet hell that would be, huh?

I mean imagine it: spending every second devoted to willful body control, side-of-your-eye attention, and intense command of attitude, vocabulary, and mannerism. It would be like a forty-year-long movie you could never act your way out of. It would be like digging your own grave with a tiny spoon and knowing that the only time you will ever get to add a little differential in your life, it will be too late. They will be putting you in the very grave you wasted your life digging.

The vain of the planet make us suffer in more ways than we can ever imagine. They make us examine all kinds of shit: what they are wearing, what you are wearing, how they look, how you look, how you feel about how they look, how they feel about how you look, how you feel about how they feel about how you look—Jesus Mary and Joseph, does this vicious whirlwind of fantasy ever subside? When all of these social factors are taken as a whole, it all boils down to one simple equation: you (x) = them cubed. They will make you feel so inadequate it becomes difficult to remember how you were able to button your own fly that morning.

As major as that sounds, there is a minor inconvenience to consider. Being an asshole does not necessarily make you a sinner. It makes you a simple hole in an ample ass. Those of us who can handle it simply deal by sauntering off to the bathroom to giggle at these sorry flakes of speck. We also tell others about you, thereby spreading the ridicule as far as we can until somewhere in Guam a rat meat salesmen chuckles under his dirty breath at a YouTube clip that someone made called "Douche Shreds," which is a video of you with someone else's voice saying "Look at me, I am a fucking douche!"

Get the picture, kiddies? People who put themselves in human trophy cases catch an incredible amount of bullshit. Now, whether they care or not, they get as much disdain as they dish out. The circle of life remains complete. The lion eats the antelope, the lion dies and becomes the grass, and then the lion/grass becomes antelope shit.

Anyway, vanity makes people do strange things that are as hilarious as the things they do when they are angry. I used to date a girl who drove by the same bank in the same small town for years, even if the bank was out of her way. Why? She wanted to see herself driving her car in the super long picture window that ran the length of the building. That is a true story; it is also why I used to date her. You can only live in someone else's world for so long before you tell them to hurry up and throw the fucking ring into the fires of Mount Doom. Get it over with; death is preferable to incessant primping.

* *

Vain people are really just snobs.

The other side of this shiny coin is that vanity can make people feel like shit. How does that work? Vanity makes you feel like shit when you do not feel you look as good as you should.

You may think this is a lack thereof, but I disagree. I think people with low self-esteem and terrible self-images are the most vain because they cannot love themselves for what and who they are. Damned if you are hot and damned if you are not—is that not a seriously fucked up thing to go through? I guess I am vain after all because I believe in my heart that I am ugly, misshapen, and completely unappealing. If only I were a little bit taller. . . .

Now most people misplace their vanity by zeroing in on one thing and ignoring the whole. Vanity is self-obsession on a base level. Like envy, it is a personal competition with everything and everyone around you. Two vain people cannot inhabit the same space. It will turn into Thunderdome in seconds, leaving disparaging comments and daggerlike stares on the battlefield like the Civil War. When two people so involved in themselves face off, it makes Gettysburg look like a game of slapjack. Do yourself a favor: Avoid this confrontation like a case of crabs in a dormitory. You will walk away with claw marks, bruises, and caked with blood, resembling a survivor from a *Nightmare on Elm Street* movie.

Then again, reverse vanity makes you just as combative. How many times have you gone fishing for a compliment about a part of your appearance you knew was gorgeous? "I just wish these jeans fit better" or "Do these shoes go with this gun?" Come on, you know you look good, at least you should know you look good. In fact, vanity is not a sin until it makes people sin to satisfy the Eternal Internal Guise Fight. Not only does vanity make men capable of lying, but it also makes women force men to lie to them. If you wrote the laws of vanity on some scratchy black chalkboard in a beat-up basement research center, they would read as such:

1) When the unstoppable force of a woman's will meets the immovable object of a man's desire for peace and quiet, you get pure vainglorious lies.

2) When a woman's kinetic energy is applied to the static energy of man, you get an extra five minutes to get that same woman out the door in order to be on time for dinner.

Sometimes vanity is just plain verboten. When was the last time you asked your drinking buddies if your hair looked all right? Have you ever broached the question of weight with the guys on your bowling team? Guys are mostly oblivious to real vanity; in fact, if their pants still fit and their underwear is clean, they cannot be bothered with that girly stuff. It certainly explains the nose hair and the forests growing in the darkest regions of their crotches. If there is not too much funk coming off of it, guys will wear it. If it is neither blush, salmon, bashful, cinnamon, or any other shade of pink, straight men will pull it on and push out the door. Do not misunderstand me—we are just as vain as anybody else. We are just not that good at it. It would certainly explain why we look so uncomfortable when we actually try to dress up and look appealing.

Women, however, are devoted to the art of *silent vanity*. They are fine with the way they look and feel, but they just need you to be on the receiving end of their vocalized inner monologue for the rest of their (and your) life. Where guys can get out of bed, rinse off, fumble for some piece of clothing that is not so offensive, and head out for the day, women are like the armed forces on D-Day. They rise at dawn. They wash for hours. They spend an afternoon on their hair and an evening on their makeup. They plan outfits like uniforms. Everything must match and everything must be perfect. If one thing does not come out the way they imagined, their day is ruined. Good luck trying to get a crumb of enthusiasm out of your significant other: All they can think about is the bang that got away from the rest of the hairdo herd. Even if the whole ensemble goes according to plan, you will be bombarded with these fateful words for at least forty-eight hours: "Do I look alright?" This will be peppered with follow-ups such as, "Are you sure?" or "Really?" It will feel like a telemarketer doing his damnedest to get you to subscribe to *Walking Weekly*, but the best you can do is spin the vanity volley back onto the court and miss on purpose. Let her win—you never had a chance to begin with.

Vanity is responsible for getting a lot of bad clothing into the national consciousness. You do not believe me? One word: bellbottoms. The most vain people are the ones who have nothing to be vain about. Supermodels look like they are made out of thin bits of driftwood. Most male models look like they could be girls if they were not forced to grow those shitty beards, and even then it is suspect. Fashion designers dress like what Timothy Leary used to see from all the acid he took. The only differences between a freak and a fashion guru are IQ and a Twitter page.

Not real enough? Okay, vanity is telling someone you love them just to gain some sort of trust because you believe you can change them and make them better. You know something, the more I think about this one, the more I think it is fun. I would love to just blame that shit on fictional characters from some Ryan Reynolds flick, but I have felt the barrel of that gun pushed against the back of my head a few more times than I am happy to admit. When a personality does not even come close to living up to the hype of that person's internal movie trailer, you should run, not walk, to the nearest exit. Things like that are the reasons why divorce is up, romance is down, and life has a hint of shit in its aftertaste when it comes to love. But every once in a while you get proven wrong, and when you do it feels great.

Back to vanity: Is it me or do vain people look a lot like puppets? They have exaggerated movements, most have funny voices, and they really want you to keep your attention focused in their direction, but only from the neck up. That is just like old episodes of *Sesame Street*: "A is for *Asshole*! Ha ha ha!!" Yeah, I crack myself up a lot more than I crack anybody else up, but that is okay. At least I am smart enough to get my own jokes. Vain people will crib quotes from famous folks in an attempt to seem "in" and edgy without having a fucking clue what they are talking about. Half the time they only say things because it could seem sweet through the sound of their voice. Meanwhile, people with half a brain would love to choke all their air out.

Self-importance can really be a pain, but I still say it is neither a sin nor is it deadly. Sure, it is a trait that can be hazardous to your health—people always want to hurt the fuckface at the party—but vain people do not kill people unless they can look good doing it. And those are just too many things for a vainglorious brain to handle at the same time. That would be like teaching an Arabian horse to fire a rocket launcher with its teeth while it stamps out its own age with its hooves. It may work in a National Lampoon movie, but in real life, thank goodness, it is simply not the way it works. Well, shit, I take that back—I guess you could drive off the road when you are primping yourself in your car mirrors, but I doubt the scriptures had that in mind when they meant "deadly." All they had back then were goat carts, and goat carts did not include side mirrors until 1957.

*   *

Sometimes vanity is in the eye of the beholder, and judgments like that make for bad gossip. Assuming someone is full of his or herself is just as bad as being full of yourself. I am sure there are good people out there who have these rumors following them around like paparazzi half the time. So why do people desperately try to tear people down all the time? Envy is a great reason. Jealous saps try to find any weakness in the armor so they can feel a little better than the other does. But does that not require just as much energy as building yourself to a place where you do not care about other people's statures? The mind boggles. It is like a Republican and a Democrat debating how to fight inflation and recession. One thinks you should dole out free money in tax cuts to people to encourage them to spend it on homegrown products, thereby stimulating the economy. The other one thinks you should instead use the money to start public programs, thereby creating jobs for the unemployed and filtering the money back into the economy. Who is right? Better yet, which way is easier?

I know several vain people in my line of work. I also know people who would have every right to be vain and they are not. I am only human; I have my moments of putting myself on a pedestal. But for the most part, I just try to do the best work I can with the time I have. Those others, those bodies who think the world revolves around them, they will claw halfway to make everyone under them feel like the top is impossible. They will shower themselves in praise and find new ways to reward mediocre results. They will crow on a fence until someone throws a fucking boot at them. They will never stop because if they do, what else do they have?

And there is the truth of it: the fear. It is the fear of being out-run when the bullets are flying. It is the fear of being eaten by a shark before you can reach the shallows. It is the fear of being the constant stranger: never being recognized, reconciled, or re-warded. It makes good cops dirty, thieves wealthy, and sinners worthy. We all worship at the Great Tit, hoping for an extra few seconds of suckle before the pipes run dry, before we get to feel full and happy. We might as well have blood and skin under our fingernails because we have all left our marks on the ones we held back in order to hold our own.

Fear makes us buy stupid shit advertised by paid program-ming. If these half-hour commercials are good at anything, it is selling us crap at 4 a.m. we never needed. But by appealing to our shoddy sense of self, we are left clamoring for things like the Ab Circle or the Power Juicer. We get conned by paid models who are too busy flexing their muscles to deliver their lines con-vincingly. And yet they are able to convince us. How the hell does that work? Guys with deeper tans than the soldiers of the French Foreign Legion, guys with British accents, fast-talking guys with keen N'Sync headsets who are prone to violence against prostitutes—all these "qualified" men are really would-be actors, shilling paraphernalia based on an infallible concept: Whether buyers know it or not, they hate themselves and it is a matter of time before they realize they don't need all this clut-tered nonsense. From the Bowflex to the Thighmaster, inven-tive minds have dedicated themselves to making sure that if we do not think there is anything wrong with us, they will let us know. Service with a smile leads to grief with a grimace, all so the particular product that you were made to feel like "you could not live without" can now gather dust within three months.

I have also noticed that vain people with no money act differently than vain people with lots of money. The poor get in fist-fights to prove their worth; the rich just marry different celebrities. But pettiness knows no tax bracket or zip code, no borders or boundaries. It could very well be the one "sin" that is communist, libertarian, and capitalist. If you have the right gear and you give great beard, you too can be the darling of the anti-bourgeoisie. When everybody sucks, so much for the class system. You can paint that shit any shade of Mao red you want—it is the universal qualm. All it takes to set it off is a little subtle push.

It was 2001 and I was playing a show at the L.A. Forum with Slipknot. I was wandering around the backstage area, watching how pompous people can become when they are convinced someone is watching. They were right I guess—somebody was watching. Unfortunately for them, it was me. And slowly but surely I was turning into a disgusted drunken asshole. I was cornered on all sides by braggarts, bimbos, and bastards. They were everywhere I looked. They were everywhere I was not. They were in my space and I did not like it. It was around that point that I found myself in a situation. There was a certain famous rock star trying to hold court at my show. I will not say his name because it would just be one more fucker trying to sue me and I have better things to do with my time. So we will just call him "Len."

Len was doing his very best to call inordinate amounts of attention to himself at a show he was not playing. I think he believed *he* was a show in and of himself, you know what I am saying? So there he was, stumbling drunkenly from hallway to hallway, followed by a gaggle of dumb-ass hookers, each one looking more haggard and disastrous than the last. I think he was truly enjoying himself, fluffing his invisible tail feathers up higher and higher until you could not even see around his entourage of pure suck. He seemed to be happy, at least as happy as this particular rascal could be, and Len made it known in the loudest voice he could muster that anyone who had a problem with the way he or "his bitches" were acting, they could say it to his face.

As luck would have it, he was standing right next to me when he was finished.

I asked him if he needed a drink and Len sneered at me, barking out booze orders for himself and his shitty harem. Then he turned around as if he were done with me. But I was not done with him. I turned him around with a calm hand and told him that if he and his rent-a-sluts wanted something to drink, he could make his way to the bar set up in the catering area. He laughed and said, "I am not going anywhere! Who are you?"

I said, "I am the guy kicking you out of my fucking show."

With that, four security guards filled in the empty area behind Len. His bimbos did not know what to do, so they left. Len stood there, getting more and more red in the face. He threw his head back and let out every vain cliché you can think of: "Do you know who I am?" "I can do what I want, I am a guest!" "I can have your fucking jobs!" There was more, but I will spare you the stupid details. Suffice it to say, he was angry because people were treating him like a regular person at a rock show. But the facts are that it was not his band playing, so he *was* a regular person at a rock show. So I had security throw his fucking ass out of my show. They were also instructed not to let him back in, no matter who tried to countermand the order. The moral of the story is watch who you fuck with; you are not always in your territory, even if you think you are.

Len has a good excuse to act like the Sultan of Shit I guess. He was a once A-List, became a B-List, now resides somewhere between D- and F-List celebrityhood, and he felt that because he felt he was in his element, he could get way with it. Then again, it was my own vanity that triggered my anger. So I guess I am just as much a fuckhead as he was. But like I said, it was my show. Right? No? Aw, shit. Honestly, I just wanted to prove a point. I mean I *was* in L.A., and that place is fraught with frivolous feeling. So to hell with the overabundance of underachievers; this should be a world where those of us with the strength and talent go exactly where we want as fast as our dreams can carry us. The best quote I ever heard was Kevin Smith talking about how people get ahead in L.A.: "In L.A., people just fail upward." That is painfully accurate and it makes me sick, but I am still here so it cannot always be that way. There is still a contingent of discontents who would rather fight for every crumb than whine for the leftovers. Shit may roll downhill, but when everyone has gas, you can smell it everywhere once it rises.

Metallica are a perfect reason to never give up hope. They are one of the greatest and most consistently creative bands on the planet. Sure, you may not agree with some of the musical choices they have made—even I was scratching my head about "Hero of the Day"—but they had the drive, the intelligence, and the fucking huge balls to do what they wanted with their career. Oh, and one more thing, you would be hard-pressed to find a band that does more for their fans than they do. They are still brilliant, even all these years after I first discovered them in my friend Che Schmitt's basement, and they still have the fucking balls to say and do what they want.

"Dad?"

"Yes, son?"

"When I grow up, I want to be in Metallica!"

"Sure thing. Did you take out the trash?"

What is it about fathers and trash day? I know, you do not have to remind me. I am about six years from that very same conversation with my kids. That is fine with me. I look forward to it.

* *

Irony, as always, surrounds each of the so-called Deadly Sins. As I have said, rage is fairly funny. Envy and greed leave you with nothing, and gluttony leaves you hungry for more. Lust fills us with emptiness, and sloth takes more effort than you could ever imagine. Vanity makes us ugly. It leaves you alone in a multitude. It whispers until all you hear are poison tongues. It will destroy everything you have until you are engulfed in ashes. It will twist your hope into a murder of crows. Then it will peck your eyes out so you can see nothing.

Fuck me, that was heavy. Maybe it is a sin after all. Nope, I'm still not convinced: Just because it makes us act like selfish cowards does not mean we are selfish cowards. We must take responsibility for our actions at some point, or someday soon there will be nothing left to blame. Humans are empty glasses with vast reservoirs of endurance. We can beat anything in our way, as long as someone stands in the way of the mirror to distract us. We are so caught up in ourselves. Between pushing up cleavage and wetting down cowlicks, it is a wonder we have time to wipe ourselves properly. St. Jude is the patron saint of lost causes. But no cause is lost if there is still one person devoted to it. So Jude might as well be the patron saint of us all.

The devout are vain in thinking they know any better than we do. I mean, let's face it: We are all mice on the wheel just trying to get a lick from that infernal water bottle. Just because they believe they have the Bat number to the Bat phone wired to God's palace in Fort Lauderdale, that does not mean they have any more answers than we do. They just pretend they do. Good for them. I hope they get that part in the Wendy's commercial.

I will always be fascinated and repulsed by this sultry sense of personality. I guess if I were a little bit shallow and a little less hungry, I would not be addicted to KFC. But as terrible as I feel afterward, I love the things I love and that is that. Doing what is right by you is a slippery slope to doing right by others, and that is a point of view the truly self-obsessed cannot abide by. Helping and sharing not because you are on camera but because you want to do something for others is just about as far from the vanity train as you can get. So tell me: What is stopping them? I think if they had one pure stimulus cross their emotional compound, they would be forced to send the guards in with dogs and mace. The ability to drop whatever it is you are doing and chime in for your neighbor is a luxury the sociopaths cannot afford with any credit card in their deck. It takes too much out of them to do something so small, and that makes them small people. And there are small people everywhere.

You would think they would feel bad, but you assume they feel. You would think they would try to correct their course, but you assume they care. This is nothing more than a clock that works and reads backward. Just when you think the alarm will wake most of us up, it lulls you back to sleep. The Beautiful Ones—they hurt you every time, as Prince once sang. Their minds were made up the second somebody gave them negative approval. Things like malice and vindication are not even in their little black books—again, you assume they care. They do not. They are only interested in what steps inside their one-foot by one-foot diameter. In other words, if they are not exclusive, they are not included.

Then again, times and people change, but the world never does. It keeps spinning, no matter who it revolves around in that moment. So my advice is simple: Do not waste your breath until you see the whites of their flags. It takes too much to deal with them, even more to pity them, and exactly $25 more to pay for anything they involve you in. You have enough to worry about. Let the pretty people talk themselves into debt for a change, huh? More has been made out of less, and they are walking, talking, fucking proof. I will wait forty-five minutes for most to figure it out, then I leave it up to them. But it was always up to them. I just let them try to figure it out with someone around— they always do their best work when someone is paying attention. That is vanity, right there: If you are looking, they are heroes. The minute you turn away, you are treated like a hooker on her birthday—you look like shit and you never changed clothes. Trust your instincts, hail Mary, and remember one thing: We all look the same after eight shots of Jack Daniels, even the ones who never changed that much from shot number one.

What time you got, bartender?

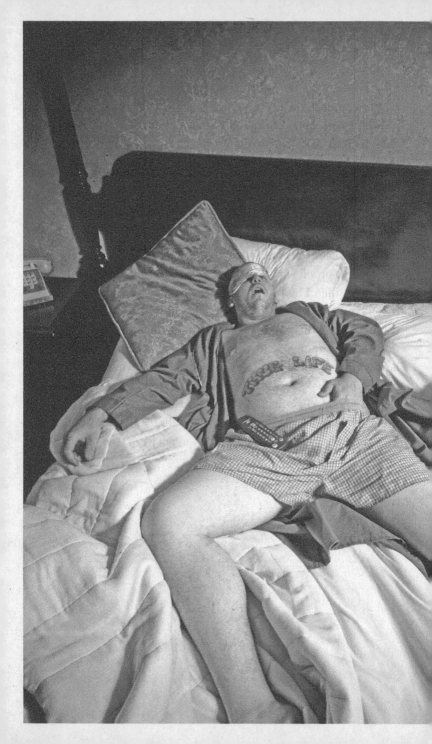

Three-Toed Sloth

Sloth . . .

Are you fucking kidding me?

Sloth?

He was the guy from *The Goonies* with the crooked face and fucked-up chick-lets, right?

Sloth!

I cannot believe I even have to write this fucking chapter, let alone defend it.

Sigh.

Okay, here we go. . . .

Sloth for the layman is laziness, albeit extreme laziness. Some might say it is more complicated than that. But really it is merely being lazy. It is that simple: no weapons, no drugs, no fucking . . . just laying there. It is doing nothing, pure, unadulterated true-blue sweet sassy American nothing. It is the vacuum of the human propensity for innovation, the other end of busy. Sloth

is absence in attendance. Sloth is the leech on the heart of ingenuity. He also loved Chunk and helped stop the Fratellis, which
was kind of heartwarming because he *was* a Fratelli, but he
helped the kids get away and held the rock so the kids could escape and . . .

If I were a real man, I would leave you with ten blank pages.
Or maybe just type this out using only one finger. I could take
pictures of myself doing so as proof. Holy living fuck, that would
take me forever. I would have to cancel all kinds of shit, like my
fencing and clog dancing classes. I do not think that is an option;
I am all-state in clog dancing. But imagine it, me in all my glory,
lying prostrate on my bed, curled up in my Spiderman Underoos
and my leopard-print Snuggie, aimlessly punching the keys with
my index finger, or better yet my middle finger. That is some
slothful shit. But because I am a loquacious blowhard, I will rant
for a while. I did not earn the nickname Great Big Mouth for
nothing, and hey, at least I am not being lazy. So I guess I will
put some fucking pants on and get to work.

This is one of those concepts that just straight bother me on
both sides of the debate. On one hand, yes, it is not good to be
a wistful fuck with no drive and no dreams. If we were all just
slovenly pigs, we would have been conquered by aliens or at
least by Canada years ago. Alaska would just be another frozen
province near the Pacific Ocean. But on the other, what is wrong
with doing dick with your time every now and then? Are we expected to be seminal broke-back creatures of industry, trying
frantically to grab a deep breath to savor before going back to
the grind? And why is it a deadly sin? Why is it such a turnoff
to turn off the engines once in a while? Who can you possibly
hurt by running on reserve power?

The argument can be made that being lazy does nothing for
the people around you and your family by and large. You can

also say that the world is a much better place because people get out of their habitual holes. As the saying goes, idle hands are the devil's playthings. So by virtue of listlessness, diabolical comeuppance can really only come from do-nothingness. Now personally, I could not give a fat fisted lady on pay-per-view if someone chooses to be slothful or not, just as long as my French fries are in the bag when I exit the drive-through. But some take it to a level that requires so much effort that it cannot be considered slothfulness by its very definition. Like Bill Cosby said, "It takes hard work to keep from working." If Daddy Huxtable said it, that is good enough for me.

So let's start with all the inventive things that we would not have in our lives without a little kind-hearted sloth to play with: hammocks, La-Z-Boys, waterbeds, motorized Rascals, those grabby things they make for people with short arms, microwaves, beer hats, Lazy Susans, that new-fangled set of fingernail clippers that has more attachments than a Swiss Army knife, extra value meals (actually, fast food in general would only be a working mother's wet dream), auto tuning, automated car washes—Are you starting to see a pattern? Without a sense of sloth, the remote control would not exist. Without sloth, we would all be busy doing standard-issue horse shit with time that could be better spent text voting for the next American Idol dipshit.

And yet people are horrified by inactivity. They condemn those lay-about fuckers who take a load off and do their very best to appear busy at all times, by any means necessary. Is it that frightening to be doing fuck all? I do not understand it, but I have another one of my controversial theorems. And much like Raymond Chandler, it just might blow the lid off of this kooky little mystery. I used the very best techniques and technology to come to this earth-shattering hypothesis: silly putty, moon sand,

and those blow pens you can order on Cartoon Network. Before you say anything, my son left that shit out, and instead of cleaning it up, I put it to work. Do not judge me. Anyway, after crunching all the data, this is where I am on the subject.

I believe this all started with comfy pajamas.

Think about those nice and beat-up flannel PJ bottoms you reserve for Saturday morning coffee and Sunday game days. There is no one more malleable to little or no movement than a person just straight chilling in their jammy-jams. I have to say, that shit is appealing as all get out. All you need after that is a robe made of dead towels and slippers that were once stuffed animals. Luckily I have both. I am not trying to put down your personal sleepwear in the slightest, as there are many advantages to having underwear and pants made of the same fabric. But flannel, corduroy, terrycloth—these things are built by Buddha, truly. Please do not plot any recriminations against me—after all, you guys are the ones decked out head to toe in underpants, man.

Honestly, the origins of this "sin" are very simple. In ancient times, people were expected to work all week and rest on the Sabbath, or Sunday. We were meant to till and sow sun up to sun down, making more for the rest of us to pass about. These were the days when burning bushes spoke to hippies and it took a village to raise an idiot. God forbid you tried to take a Tuesday off to watch your kid's Bocce Ball game, or whatever they used to play in the 1960s (that was before my time). Never mind if it was because you were proud of the outfit your meager wife stitched together using nothing but bark and rock. They would more than likely cast you out as a witch or, worse yet, a liberal. So the roots of sloth lay in the virtues of menial labor, I guess. It seems like social judgment knows no time line.

But my argument is that this is just not a modern-day sin. Sloth has gone the way of Friendster and eight-track tapes.

These days no one can really be slothful; cell phones are leashes and technology leaves no stones unturned. There is nowhere to hide today. There are only places to catch your breath. Hell, even people just sitting on their ass are doing something. Look at me for instance: sitting on my big leather couch writing a book that most of you motherless shits will most likely download and dump on your Kindles. But I am busy nonetheless. And you will all be busy getting nerdy for something you could very easily have gone out and bought with a coffee at a book shop. You will be online or receiving scans that come directly to your home fax machine or texting or tweeting, whatever the fuck that shit means. You see, we are all a little bit busier than "God" expected we would be. This world has gone south of crazy and north of ordinary. This spinning blue marble is a fucking chaotic anthill, and I can almost bet on the fact that most everyone is doing his or her part to feed the collective. As the blank parts of the map were being colored in, we were connecting our network of dots to support a growing need to get shit done.

Sloth in this day and age requires more expended energy than being "slothful" qualifies for. It means canceling all kinds of shit: appointments, work, any kind of sports activity you might be involved in, a date, a wax, a happy ending—it all has to go if you want an annual Sloth Day. Okay, maybe not the handjob—that can only make you sleepy and improve your slothfulness—but everything else must go. It becomes a fire sale for the next twenty-four hours. And that, just by definition, makes it anything but sloth. When the hands at the end of your wrists no longer know control or restraint, you are neither slothful nor well. You are a tool for the grist of God. Or Sam—whatever your boss's name happens to be.

I work constantly. When I am not working, I am trying to raise my kids. When I am not raising future anarchists, I am working on other people's tomfoolery. My cycle is powered by jet fuel. Hey man, you just never know when the quarters are going to run out while you are riding the electronic elephant outside the toy store. Sloth to me is not a sin, but it is quite offensive. The simple matter that some people cannot find at least a little bit of something to do with their time is a miraculous travesty to me. If I were not able to do as much as I could with the time I have, I would go stir crazy. You would find me shaving my nuts in the fountain by the airport—you know, the one the employees all smoke around. My compulsion may come from serious childhood issues, but I refuse to assume that this could last forever. When I die, I want to leave behind enough proof so people remember I was alive in the first place. High-five your nearest coworker because that is true immortality. The price of sloth is the seat nearest the door to the linen closet.

So, because of my manic frantic state of panic, I have spent the better part of fourteen years traveling. I spend stupendous amounts of time on planes, buses, cars, trains, ferries, and other forms of transportation. I work on all of the above. I have become the ever-present cock smear on the plane, the guy who has his shit ready before he even gets to security. So sloth does not exactly find itself susceptible to growth in the Petri dish that is my life. I move too fast to let the moss gather momentum. My temptation is *more work*. And I am still trying to figure out what the hell is wrong with me. I do not foresee any test results in the near future.

I used to complain about too much work. Now my voracity knows no bounds. I will drive myself into the ground before I allow myself to get too comfortable on the couch. Besides, too many of my friends have broken my furniture—why do you think I am writing this fucking book in my kitchen? Anyway, vacations are nice and there is always time to watch *Dexter*, but if I am not working toward fifteen goals at once, I am not a happy camper. In fact, it drives me bat shit when I could be doing something and I am not able to for whatever reason. Funeral homes should really have Wi-Fi; I am sure I am not the only one who thinks that or who has complained to the owner about it. How am I supposed to spend my time while people are praying? I could be replying to e-mails!

Yet there are still people with defeatist attitudes and lack of will who think life owes them a favor. Life owes you nothing; you owe yourself everything. I learned that shit on my own walking home from school one day. There is no guarantee you will be around tomorrow. The wheels of a rickshaw could fly off and take out your entire face, leaving you looking like you lost a fight with a rabid badger. You could wake up in the morning and, while you are still groggy, accidentally brush your teeth with toilet bowl cleaner—you are just getting around to scraping the eye boogers out of your oculars and now you are dead in a really stupid way. Anything is possible in a world that takes Sarah Palin this seriously. So get off of your ass, take a shower, and fix that fucking cabinet door in the bathroom!

* *

Being a man and studying history the way I have, it seems that carrying a concealed penis meant you were just expected to work from day one. No time for sloth when you are doing the jobs of ten Amish barnburners, right? Women have had their share of chores but not until the last eighty years have they taken it upon themselves to lean into a pitch or two so we can have at least one person on base. I know, for the longest time men frowned on this and even legislated terms that kept women in check. Men are terrified of change and they cannot handle it when Ethyl can do anything they can do. But that did nothing to change the fact that men are expected to work for a living and women are given the option. You fought hard, ladies: Light up a Virginia Slim and celebrate. For you, it was a battle for equality, respect, and a chance to build something for a lifetime. For guys nothing changed. There was no empathy for men; we did not hold rallies or support parades that resounded with the idea that if women want to work then men should get a day off. To this day we are still genetically and socially pressured to do whatever is necessary, to put in the time and the effort.

I am a firm believer in equal rights and I have seen firsthand that women are often more capable than men when it comes to being prepared for anything. While women were fighting for the right to stand and be counted, men were just fighting. Men are the mules of our species and women are the drivers, the herders, the overlords of a world in dire need of direction. I am very proud of the leaps we are taking to bring the sexes head-to-head on the playing field. It is just a shame that the hard work that most men have put in for years has gone unnoticed.

I have noticed sins have no potency without vessels of action. The strange thing is that when these sins are used in combinations, they are so much more aggressive. Our forebearers might have known this, but they sure as hell did not put it in their book. So you are left trying to do the math, and that leaves you with 50–50 Oxy/Cotton. Good times on weak wings—fly while you can because the ride is not cheap. There are layers to cakes and labors too cheap to mention. If you do not have the savvy to know which is which, you are certainly going to earn the scar on your mouth. Tell them you cut yourself shaving.

Back to my point: Envy and greed can breed either champions or martyrs. Lust and rage can make you a monster or Don Juan. As such, sloth with an infusion of gluttony simply gives birth to drug addicts and wastes of flesh. I truly believe that sloth is harmless left to its own devices. But in tandem with other forces it can cause damages not ever imagined or experienced. Sloth and rage makes an expert. Sloth and greed makes a brother-in-law. Sloth and lust will leave you surfing porn in a basement with a neck beard and a poop sock, bothering your mother to buy more Pop-Tarts the next time she hits the grocery store. In a lot of ways, it is a "gateway sin": It leads you away from the ground-work of the original problem and sets you in chains against a backdrop designed for penance and shame. You can have the best intentions in the world, but if you do nothing, you are noth-ing. It is a harsh glare to shed that kind of light, but in my heart that is pure reality for me. How does the quote go? "Evil tri-umphs when good men do nothing." This is the downside to the longevity of sloth. It is an exit on a highway that leads to the worst parts of town.

Like vanity, sloth can be an enabling type of viral distress, a way of life that is way off course. It is a simple case of strong people forgetting their nut sacks on the corner of the dresser before they leave the house in the mornings. It can take away fantastic thoughts and replace them with consumer taglines. A mind is left bereft when it is nothing more than a tool of regur-gitation. You have to think for yourself, but we all have to be taught to do so, and if you are not paying attention, you will pay for it later. Sloth's blind eye is your deafening silence; touch the stones before you go so you have luck pulling yourself out of hell. We are only what we allow ourselves to be. If there is no permission, there is no pursuit. The only hell I recognize is the one we build with our own two hands, and that is a job even a slothful person can handle.

But sins do not sin for themselves. They are just the subjects to our predicates, the mystery cream in our Oreos. We can be bad all on our own, but we need someone else to talk the cops out of giving us a ticket. It is the habit of the Church to find new scapegoats for our actions. Maybe that was the whole reason they were put in charge to begin with—so they could find us ways to alleviate how fucked we felt. Hey, it makes sense: If there is a group of people who can create savory myths out of thin air, it is the Church. But if we all set our feet on the ground and took the beating once in a while, we would see it is just more evidence of what we *do*. Human beings fuck up all the damn time, so get fucking used to it. Save your complaints—I am the DMV of giving a squeaky shit about your troubles. Life sucks, so grab a straw and suck it.

I believe how we feel is just as responsible as who we are when it comes to what we do. Depression can fill our lungs with lead and bury us alive under a mountain of ennui. Dwelling on past mistakes gets you nowhere in a taxi where the meter never stops running. I once spent a whole week in my pajama bottoms, tethered to my couch, ready to let oxygen off the hook. I did not want to move, I did not want to breathe, I did not want to feel, and I did not want to think. I just wanted to wallow in my bullshit until someone came to take the pain away. The thing I did not realize was the only person who had the power and wherewithal to do so, ironically enough, was the one living in his pajama bottoms and wasting time on the couch. For those of you not paying attention, that person was me. Since then I have never let myself get too far off of the reservation. I take what I can and dump the rest before it gets overwhelming. Life will give you buckets of blood sometimes, enough to drown your sorrows but too much to float on. So you have to find a way to paint the walls with what is left over. You have to empty the vats before it becomes too much because we all know it is perennial. It never stops, so never stop trying.

By the by, I am aware that some people fight off any slothful traits with pharmaceuticals, chemicals, and barbiturates. I am very happy to report I have no need for any of these dangerous stimuli. All I need is a pot of coffee—a pot of coffee, a mouth-piece, and a tranquilizer gun for when the froth becomes too much for the roommates. Throw on the java and watch me go. I can wade through my musings like an armored tank division. I had my fill of uppers and coke in my teens. I left the thrills of the 7 percent solution in the death throes of my young adult-hood. Besides, if you have a craving for a drug that kills your bon-ers and drives you banana shit, you have more problems than finding ways to fill your dance card, friend. What the hell are you going to do with your time? Beat up monks and dry hump Chryslers? Does any of that make *any* sense to anyone? I would rather be bored for a little while than sell out my tenders for a pick-me-up. I am naturally hyper as well, so I am all set. What a super-fucked situation to find yourself in: all spruced up and no one to blow. Make mine massive, because there are worse things to have to deal with than your own imagination. It is just a ques-tion of how long it takes for your scrotum to pull apart like a tire patch set. That's one "Just Say No" ad I would kill to direct.

But I am just one guy with an overactive adrenalin gland. There are no universal rules to how a body works. Maybe some of you *do* need a few extra hands to get that boost for action. You run the risks in a race against yourself. You just have to know which way the starter pistol is pointing so you do not get your face blown off. In fact, most people who get ahead have not done shit to do so. Look at most celebrity children. Now, I am very sensitive to this because I have children of my own and I know someday they might suffer in this comparative light. But most other famous broods fucking bask in it and are just fine doing nothing more. Give them a trust fund and a lifetime of margaritas and they are all set—no want or need to contribute to the human collective. With enough coverage on TMZ and E! Entertainment, they make sure that the world as a whole covets their "reality" show as well. But have you ever noticed how every reality show has an army of producers making sure the "reality" is exciting? These people cannot even take care of their own lives without a director to tell them how to shit.

So between sloth and envy, these lucky fucks have it made. I wonder if their mothers realize how charmed their vaginas are. They spit out nouveau riche knock-offs like yeast infections. In the galactic crapshoot, they win the big bear no one can get in the backseat of their cars. It must really be a burden to be born with everything and left with very little. Most rich people I know are uninteresting piles of havoc. The only real thing they have ever had to experience was being chastised for trying to steal money from a wishing well; they were convinced all money was theirs.

What really chaps my Irish ass is when these sloth-bucklers have the audacity to complain when people try to fuck with their ride: "Oh, my problems, my problems." How about you get off of your dead asses and do a decent day's fucking work for a change, you ungrateful dick smokers? When you are living a gilded life, what in the hell do you have to complain about? Sit in your fucking cages and shut the fuck up. Well, I guess my rage is flaring up, and it could be the Herculean amounts of coffee I have been chugging since this morning. But even if I was not jacked up on French roast, I would still be adamant about my hatred for these jackasses who cannot seem to raise up enough to keep from sitting on their own hands. The fact that they decry those who have worked hard, if not harder, than not only themselves, but more than likely their own parents is enough for me to want to kiss them on the foreheads with a baseball bat. So pass a note to those whining dildos: Do something worth our admiration and maybe we will give you a call. Until that time, go fuck your living selves.

Yeah, I have some issues. So what? At least I am busy, right? I am every bit as bad as the apples I am juicing. You will never get me to admit it in court, though. There is something to be said about still recognizing your own stink, if you get my drift. Just because I empathize does not mean I sympathize. These people never slept on the street. They never ate garbage, and they never lived through a cold night in their entire lives. Do not expect me to give a rosy red clit rubbing if one of their trophy pets dies or their fake tan goes from brown to khaki. I would not chum the Pacific with their leftovers to draw in sharks. If that makes me a bad person, then fuck yeah, give me all the black clothing you got and a damsel in distress to tie to some railroad tracks. Nah, that is too dated—I will just run over with a rented Segway any skinny stupid blonde debutantes who get in my way.

I am the other end of the swimming pool. I am the reason I cannot sleep at night. Why do the freeloaders bother me so much? Maybe it is because I have never claimed more than I have earned. Maybe it is that I cannot and probably will never relate to a life spent in almost utter absentia. All I have known in my life is work and progress. All I have been shown is that you must make yourself a legend in order to scratch your name on the Great Oak. So when "entitled" morons get thrown book deals and movie roles and unmerited praise, I hang my head and fight back too many vicious tirades to count on my phalanges. When I see one of them embroiled in controversy, I feel the same way I do when a Kennedy dies. That may be a little dark, but I have nothing in common with a hierarchy that has been accused in the past of funding a lifestyle that has been debased, tawdry, and counterfeit. We can do better, or at least we can hope for better. They cannot: They are stuck being gold-plated, dim-witted, and asinine. You would have thought that with all that money, they could have hired someone to tell them that marrying cousins does wonders for the gene pool.

I wish I knew a fart joke to lighten the mood right now, but so much for pathos. Tell you what—I will get a grip when they get a clue. What the fuck can they take from me that I cannot do without? I can play and sing on any street corner and scrounge enough to buy a pack of smokes. I can scream my diabolical diatribes at open-mike nights to a packed house of seven people and be okay. What can they take? They cannot take anything from me. So I will never take back anything I have ever said. This is me scared shitless—any questions?

Maybe that is the key. Sloth plants seeds of doubt in the most fertile fields of man. I have no doubts in my abilities or talents.

I am not saying I am cocksure or full of myself. I just know what I can do. So I do it a lot. I do it whether I get paid or not. I am an entertainer at day's end, and as long as there are people lining up to see me do whatever it is I do, who the hell am I to rest on laurels that can wait until I am infirm and gray? I want the world, and that does not jibe with sloth at all. I am just not in tune with this "sin." I am still not convinced it is a sin. It is a ludicrous place in the soul that just wants to stake a claim and sit on it. I do not want to start sounding older than I am, but what the hell is wrong with that? Is that what we are left with in this country? A horde of shiftless wonders who cannot tie their shoes without looking it up on Google? I do not buy it and I would like to put whoever is selling it out of business. Old fogies go on and on about "the good old days" when honesty and sweat built an empire called the USA. I wish I had just a single memory of any of that time; maybe if I did I would not be so angry. People always say that "times are changing." But time does not change—people do. Time does what it has always done, rolling over us like waves of warm water and setting us to simmer in baths of inevitability. Time only points us in the right direction. It will never make you move on your own.

If satisfaction is the murderer of our dreams, then sloth supplies the pillows we suffocate under when we try to lower our heads to rest. It seems like such a lukewarm and harmless thing, but sloth can erode bones from the inside. It can harvest dead wheat in a land of plenty. It can rip us to pieces with the simplest action, which is doing nothing whatsoever. So to rally the troops, we must control our appetites for lush extravagance. We need to remember that although Rome was not built in a day, it was also not built with prayers and wishes. It takes people to do what the people want. Leaders come and go, but the fire of our will has burned down the greatest obstacles of our lives. We cannot give in to commonplace worries. We have to be willing to face our instincts and sort them with rationality. The battles of our generation will be fought not on the streets but in our minds, because who can ever beat us one on one?

Sins have stained the cloths of royalty and ruined the air we breathe from time to time. Sins have pulled apart rope bridges left for escape and leveled the temples we dared to worship in back when we were a little bit different and a little more the same. But banality is hardly a sin. Being benign and faltering from lack of use is really just another reminder that we are three inches farther away from each other than the last time we stopped and talked. No effort means no more flyaway hairs standing on end in acrimonious displays of disagreement. No qualms or shows of distaste means not so much blood to clean from our hands and fingernails. How many species can say with as much brutal truth as possible that by not saying or doing anything, they are keeping us from killing each other?

Our proximity keeps us honest. Our intentions keep us strangers.

*   *

When I was young, we sat on stoops and sang the evenings back into their shoeboxes so as not to lose any stars. Apartment buildings were brick villages, and around 5 p.m., those who worked came home and those who played joined them for some air. I remember barbecues and discussions, sociable symmetry on Thursday nights. Sloth was used to enjoy sun tea and potato salad until the chicken was done. Sloth was grabbing a lawn chair and talking about the preseason with 1A across the hall and 2B upstairs. This was no sin: It was *siesta*, a way of coaxing a little more life out of languid hours and good company. If sloth is deadly, then just plain lazy will put you in a coma. Iowa is a wonderful place for this type of exemption. We are the middle, but in the middle of nowhere. We seem to be a punch line to the Coasts, but we were the first to legalize same sex marriage. The whole country glues itself to our doorstep every four years for the caucuses, where political bigwigs watch the outcomes like starving hawks on a day pass. So we must be doing something better than they are, like turning slothfulness into an exotic hobby. I am a blue-collar guy with a white-collar income. Iowa gave me appreciation for everything, including the rare spare time I have.

So what do we do? I say we retire sloth to the Vatican like a superstar's number in his home stadium. They can hang it in the Sistine Chapel next to God's pointer finger, as if he is saying, "Wow, remember when something as boring as sloth was considered one of the seven deadly sins? I sure am glad Corey Taylor cleared up all that doubt for us. My, he is a handsome fellow. He truly is created in my image. Have you seen his neck? The thing is like a tree trunk, are you fucking kidding me? You would go through four axes before you made a dent!" Okay, maybe that is not the conversation your God is saying, but my God curses and thinks my neck should be declared a national treasure. No? Your loss, people.

Anyway, we could do the unthinkable and make sloth an ice cream flavor. The trouble would come when no one had the energy to taste it. We could sponsor a car in its honor: the new Ford Sloth. It would never sell all that well though . . . *because all it would do is idle!!!!!!! Ha ha ha ha ha ha!!!* That shit was real as fuck!! Did you read that? It was amazing!! You do not have to admit it. I know the truth. That shit worked on two different levels—total and utter brilliance! Ooh, we could discover a new species of plant life and incorporate sloth into its Latin translation. Now we just need to find a fuzzy little fern that grows no higher than a foot off the ground, depletes the food and water all around it, and very well could be harvested and made into stuffing for organic pillows. I predict a new hot item for next Christmas.

This is proving to be the hardest chapter to write. I mean, how many different ways can you be clever talking about a state of mind that is not far from a vegetative state? I suppose there are worse things that could happen, like the earth's orbit could pull Halley's Comet into our atmosphere and hammer it into the bedrock beneath the ocean floor, flash boiling deciliters of salt water, creating tsunamis and tidal waves not seen since the earth was forming. Between the catastrophic effects of the initial impact and the resulting shifts in polarity and plate activity, I would give the earth minutes, not days. In the event that that shit happens, this is exactly what I am going to do:

I am going to corral my wife, my children, and any other family members standing close by and get them to "safety." I will then give my children hugs and kisses, grab my wife's sweet sexy ass, and head for Wal-Mart. I will pick out the nicest hammock available. I am not that big of a snob when it comes to designer colors, but it has to be super comfy and ultra-simple to set up. I will then help myself to four Texas fifths of my man, my friend, my saucy dancing partner, Mr. Jack Daniels. I will then return to my family's whereabouts, string up my hammock, and drink until impact. Just for good measure, as that heavenly body of horse fucker is plummeting toward my planet, I am going to drink a shot off of my wife's ample chest and flip that son of a bitch off as it hits the ground. Maybe I will also jump in the air as it is hitting.

Jesus stuffed-crab Christ, even in a no-win scenario, with no chance of survival, I cannot relax enough to find a way to even approach being slothful. I am a failure at fallacies. I guess I am just doomed to be on point, all the time, till that son-of-a-bitch fucking comet gets here. Yeah, I know it will never happen, but it is not the only thing hurtling through space. We are not the focal point of the universe—hell, we are not even an exit sign for the universal highway. We are more like one of the pebbles they use to cover the sides of the road. That is the size proportion we are dealing with: galactic soap scum in the big bathtub in the sky.

*   *

I am sitting here with my coffee, looking at the valley that my house in L.A. sits above, watching workmen build three different homes for people who, more than likely, are not even around. These men have been doing these jobs for months: waking us up in the morning, keeping us awake around noon, interrupting conversations in the afternoon, startling us when they come back from their lunch break, and immediately using a jackhammer. If anything, these men are very committed. And that is an apt metaphor for this whole chapter. These people show up day in, day out and set themselves to a backbreaking task, surrounded by houses full of people who probably make copious amounts of money for doing a lot of nothing. These men are on display in an open-air menagerie, adding a little more to the landscape and paying close attention to their architecture. They do not give a shit if they wake us lazy shits up or make us have to talk a little louder to hear each other. They take pride in their work even though they do it all the time, rain or shine.

There are men and women just like them all over this country, in every county, every city, and every township just outside the capital. They do the things they do because they are carrying on a fundamental tradition and a way of thought that many are convinced has been gone from America for a very long time. Trust me—I have been to every state in the Union and I see my fellow Americans hanging on. No recession can bring us down. No depression can break our resolve. There may be a percentage that throws off the bell curve, but the pros far outnumber the cons: The pros are doing more for a better world and the cons are doing time for a life spent wasted. Sloth can lead a man to crime, but it does not mean he will steal. Sloth can slow a man's progress, but it will not make him fall. If life and history have proven anything, it is that men do what they want. Some men choose to fail. Thankfully, most men choose to win.

In a place that needs constant care and takes so much energy to strengthen, sloth is left to its own devices because it cannot get a hold in this new world. We move forward on our own, treating each step not with the mentality of a triage but as a chess game. We live better by thinking ten steps ahead, anticipating every counter-move and celebrating each gain. So I say we send sloth out on the water and give it the Viking funeral it so richly deserves. It is a human trait that holds no sway over this mess of memories any longer. Our white cells have been fighting this so-called pestilence since before we were born. Just because the fight is getting easier, that does not mean we have won the title. None of us are immune to the allure of aloofness. We do not know where we are going, but we are pointed in the right direction. The challenges are where we find ourselves. The obstacles are now scenery for the long walk home. We can overcome anything we want because our greatest advantage is that we are all alive, and as long as we are alive, we have everything. So pick up a stick, smack at the grass, and whistle a while. There is no sin in that.

My Waterloo

It is funny how things work out sometimes.

There are proponents who maintain that we are all products of two different variables: genetics and environment. This is saying we are one part who we are born to be and one part what we are turned into through relationships, family, childhood, and the rest. I happen to agree; the things we go through make us who we are. Our yins and yangs are usually nothing to boast about, but in this life, being extraordinary has to take a collision of talent, drive, and passion mixed with a certain amount of dysfunction and insanity, an almost-perfect storm that makes one person a star and another just a plain old fuck up. In other words, it takes a lot to be a lot.

But I want to take it a step farther. In addition to genes and surroundings, I believe everyone in the world has two places in their hearts: the city you are born in and the city that defines you. For most people, it could be the city their parents raised them in and the city where they went to college. For me, both were in the same state. I was born in Des Moines, Iowa, on December 8, 1973. However, starting in 1984, my soul was formed in a darker place.

Come off Highway 29 before you hit the tiny little mix-master over by the Crossroads Mall and you will see Greenwood Park at the horn of River Forest Road. The dike by the river almost runs parallel, mirroring the curve like a geographical pair of quotation marks. River Forest takes you to Lafayette Road, a gray blacktop vein that stretches through almost four towns, combining them into a straight line of morose loneliness, despair, and intolerance. You follow Lafayette till you hit downtown—gutted, rusty, and closed in on all sides by broken cement and tragedy. Along the way you are assaulted by the remnants of a city that used to have a purpose until the businesses moved away, leaving economic devastation in its wake. High schools, railroad tracks, and dead eyes—welcome to Waterloo.

Waterloo, Iowa, and its sister towns of Evansdale, Elk Run Heights, and Cedar Falls were the backdrop of the worst moments of my life. From Jewett Elementary all the way until my final days at East High School, it was a cornucopia of racism, malicious intent, and ignorant torrents of pain. I can still feel the evil in the marrow of my spine, my bones, and my soul. I was beaten in this town. I was raped in this town. I was destroyed in this town. I almost died in this town. I was hated in this town.

So I learned to hate it right back.

Before I go any further, let me make myself very clear: This is not a reflection of the people who live there now. I have not been back in years and I am fairly out of touch with the current population. I am quite certain the folks who make up the old "319" these days are very lovely. No, my seething hate comes from the time I spent there, and my deep-seated need to escape. There is a little bitterness connected to my five years there in every line I have ever written. It stripped me of my innocence. It was where I first learned that no one is safe, not even a starving, eleven-year-old kid who only wanted to fit in, laugh, and be loved. But when you are left to the whim of the selfishness of adults, your safety and your heart go up in flames like a funeral pyre.

When no one cares, you learn to follow suit to survive.

It was in this town that all of these "sins" really hit home for me. Every one of them was an escape or an assault. It seemed I was a wanton lust monger, a glutton for punishment, a jealous, envious dick pining for recognition on any level, and a raging knot of fury all buried under blond hair and blue eyes. But I do not want to get ahead of myself. Let me set the scene for you.

My mother, my sister, and I moved to Waterloo when I was eleven years old. We had been moving around from state to state for about six months. I did not even get to finish fourth grade. After a brief and shitty stint in Florida, I was told we were going back to Iowa. I was led to believe we were going back to Des Moines, a city I was very fond of and where I still had many friends. Instead, we landed in Waterloo with my mother's then-boyfriend. We moved into a trailer court on River Forest Road, surrounded by mud and dog shit, promptly taking up residence in Lot #20. In this morose little ecosystem, #20 was the trailer in the middle of everything, five lots down from the city street and caddy corner to the big white building that apparently housed all the washing machines, a construct that was conspicuously always locked up. That building scared the hell out of my sister. For some reason, though, one time she ran away and we found her in that building. We never knew why—hell, I did not even ask. I understood the urge to run.

After a few months, my mother broke up with her boyfriend and we moved in with her brand-spanking new best friend. I will not say her name out loud because every time I do, I curse and spit, but her nickname was Corky. She was a disgusting forty-year-old power alcoholic who was balancing three men, slightly raising a daughter, and hell-bent on sucking the very light from the sun if it meant people would look to her for warmth. I know the golden rule is if you have nothing good to say about someone, say nothing at all. Well, if I had no choice but to talk about Corky for the rest of my life, I would have to take a vow of silence. Corky died of cancer about fifteen years ago, and it is the best example I have in the world to believe in karma. I have never told anyone this, but I used to make a trip every year just so I could piss on her grave. The only good thing that came out of her was her daughter Missy, who I affection-ately call my other sister to this day.

I was a child confronted with addictions and domestic vio-lence. It was Jerry Springer every night at our house. You ever want to feel powerless? Watch people you care about being hurt and know there is nothing you can do about it. The only good thing about that time in my life was I swore I would never let it happen again. The degree of ignorance and filth I was bom-barded with had absolutely no right to exist in a world that was fair, but obviously I learned the hard way that when shit hits the fan, it flies in every direction, and by the time I was fifteen, I was covered in it. There was no peace, nor was there ever any sense of security. We were just fodder at the red ends of a few rotten whims. The tables had turned in my life and not at all for the best.

I watched one of Corky's boyfriends break an entire plate of food on my mother's face. The cops showed up every other night for a domestic dispute. My sister watched Corky steal money from my mother's purse and Mom didn't believe her. We moved around constantly because of this. They told us it was just time for a change, but I knew better. You cannot have that many complaints and be allowed to stay in one place. All the while, we were beaten regularly with belts, paddles, and fists covered in low-rent turquoise rings. I still have scars on my eyelids from those rings. I got to know all four townships very well because they were my only escape, and when all you want to do is disappear, how far enough is away?

But there were other dangers besides the war at home. It sucks being the poor kid, the weak kid, the new kid, or the weird kid. I was always all four. I did not make real friends till I was in high school, and even then, they were usually kids who used to beat me up, jumping me on my way home from school. I had no one to teach me how to fight, no one to teach me to stand up for myself. My soul was a fucking bomb and my temper became the mercury switch. I wanted the fucking world to burn.

Just when I thought I was doomed to suffer forever, music saved my life.

You can say whatever you want about metal or rock or punk or old school hip hop, but at the time, the Beatles did not say a fucking thing to me. They sure as fuck were not speaking *for* me either. And Debbie Gibson was plastered all over the radio as well; plastic music was finding its legs in the '80s. Between burgeoning boy bands and meek pop rock, I needed something with a little more than bark. I needed teeth and venom. My generation was raised on Marlboro cigarettes, Metallica, and any drugs we could get our hands on. Black Flag, Slayer, Mötley

Crüe, and Public Enemy gave me the answers to all my questions. When I was ready to quit fighting, they held my fists in place.

Do not get me wrong—I am not bragging. This was survival, pure and simple.

Maybe that is at the heart of this book. What you call sins were my escape. Music and writing allowed me to unleash the wrath building up in my heart, and the speed I was taking ensured I did not have to go to sleep too long to endure the nightmares. Puberty and good cheekbones made sure I could indulge my lust. Envy and greed pushed me to look past the borders of that godforsaken hole called home, even before I realized I had some kind of talent. Gluttony showed me that I wanted it all *right fucking now*, no matter what the risks. Vanity just meant not wearing the same ripped up clothes too many days in a row. The only thing I never subscribed to was sloth. For me, sloth was the day spent sleeping off a hangover.

Shit catches up with you in the end, but when you are young, you have no expiration date. You have no idea how precarious life can be, especially when your selfish tunnel vision keeps you focused on what *you* want and nothing else. When you are wound that tightly, even hell feels like home. And why not? My so-called safety net was a mesh of mess made up of binge drinkers, druggies, and inbred horny toolbags. If anyone I used to live with gets butt hurt over that last statement, I really do not give a ragged fuck. Life sucks, so close your mouth so your teeth do not click.

So I fucked and smoked and screamed and sped my way through life. I ran rampant through dark alleys and finite futures just to end up right back where I had always been. I did not want to be a despot in a sea of fire. I did not want to be a fly in a swarm of wasps. I was different, but I wanted to be different. There is a difference: Some people try and some people just are. Martyrs will beg you to pepper them with stones; enigmas never even notice the first strike.

I was so desperate to have a friend that I ended up hanging out with an older boy whose family lived next door to us. For this book's purposes, I will call him Jason. Jason was five years older than me and was into music just like me. He even turned me onto some great bands I had never heard of before. Every day after school, I would go spend time at his place because it was safer than my own home. It was, that is, until he raped me.

As I look back now, I guess with all the bullshit going on at home, I should have been smart and savvy enough to see it coming. I was a confused scared kid who only wanted to have one person who did not hurt him in his life; he was all of those things because he was a predator and he knew that was what I wanted. So at the age of eleven, my best friend raped me in his basement. When it was over, I went home and never told a soul. Jason's house burned down a week later. His family fled in the middle of the night. The whole neighborhood was convinced that I had done it. I never saw him again.

Some scars run deep and some wounds never heal, but that sweet, sweet anger lives forever. It is what it is, and I have learned to accept it. That does not mean I am happy about it, but I learned a long time ago that holding onto the past too tightly leaves rope burns from the noose you carry around with you. I was so angry about it for so long that it became my only reason to feel. The violation takes time to let go of, but the moment gets farther away if you let go of the chain you have used to drag it behind you. Sometimes you have to be more than a survivor. Sometimes you have to move on.

We eventually moved out of Corky's place, right back to the same damn trailer park we had started in years before and right back into Lot #20. I shit you not. I was in eighth grade by then, and I finally had a group of friends who were my home away from home. They were dreamers like me, but they could only see so far. I could see the end of the universe. But how do you explain that to people who do not really care? How do you explain to someone that you are fucking searing inside and if you do not go somewhere with your life, you are going to explode? The only difference between a star and a black hole is time.

So I just tried to enjoy what I did have. We spent days on the dike by the river. You could hide there, you see. We used to build forts out of the giant white rocks that were in place to keep the river from spilling over onto people's barbecues and satellite dishes on the other side. Plus we had the forests that lined the river bank, giant trees as far as you could see. It was like *Lord of the Flies.* We learned about acid in those woods. I really do not recommend that: There's nothing worse than watching your buddy attack a tree because "it said some shit about my mother!" We chugged bottles of Robitussin, which is an unhealthy, horrible way to get high. This was years before crunk and all that syrup movement bullshit. We just knew it was going to fuck us up. But that was not all. We ate peyote and smoked ourselves blind. We baptized ourselves in chemicals and clarity. We were trying to find our faith, but all we found at the end of the day was that, by and large, we seemed to be immortal.

When we were not getting closer to nature, we invaded the suburbs, running the streets like denim banshees, high as fuck and out of control. We stormed a kid's house we did not like and did so much damage the cops showed up. The kid was *home* when we did it. We did anything, anywhere. In Evansdale, there is a park at the end of Myer, right in the middle of everything. We set every tree on fire one night and danced under the cold moon, waiting for judgment that never came for us.

We had no reason for anything because we *had no reason*. I mean, what the fuck did they expect? We were dealing with hormones and psychoses and rising prices and falling rocks and anything else that is dangerous yet completely out of our control. Sins, my ass—these were fucking hobbies. These were the only reasons to get out of bed or, in my case, the bathtub. Yeah, I slept in our bathroom for a year because there was nowhere else to sleep. I would get up in the morning, put my blanket and my pillow in the bathroom cupboard, take a shower, then get my clothes out of the hamper . . . in the same bathroom. Kicks ass, right?

Things like that make me thankful I lived to write about it.

*   *

It was not always shitty, you know. Evansdale, which is right outside of Waterloo, was where I ate a Now & Later candy for the first time. When I lived in Dewar, which is right outside of Evansdale, I learned through another group of kids that I was good at football. It is funny what you see and what you refuse to see in retrospect. I suppose I had some great times with that crazy cast of characters. There were even times when I did not feel so different from them, or they did not seem that different from me. In a way, they kept me alive. When I needed to escape, they came with me. When I needed to feel alive, they joined me.

I even started one of my first bands with those guys. But I could never trust them. Maybe that is the real lesson I took away from Waterloo: Do not trust anyone. And I learned it so well that I still have a hard time letting it go. My wife, Stephanie, is one of the greatest people I have ever met, and I still have a hard time fully trusting her. But because she is amazing, she has infinite patience. She understands and helps me every day.

I am surviving again, really. It may be a cop out, I know. But it is the biggest reason why I have this type of strength and re-solve. I refuse to give up, I refuse to die, and I refuse to lose, *ever*. It is because I remember every word, every scar, and every dirty secret. I am a mass of melodrama disguised as a life. But at least I am not a fabrication from some conference table in a nonde-script building. At least I was not put together by executives in some shitty pitch meeting who wanted an edgier artist with bet-ter cheekbones—"You know . . . for the kids!" I am everything that ever happened to me. I am real and skin and bone and alive and ready for every day I have.

And for that, grudgingly, I guess I owe Waterloo a thank you.

Thank you, Waterloo. Thank you for making me who I am. Thank you for ripping me to shreds and making me build my-self back up in the end. Thank you for setting me on fire, be-cause I used that fire to fight for everything I have ever earned. Thank you for trying so hard to destroy my innocence, so much so that I held on with fingers and nails just to keep it safe. Thank you for showing me the most brutal realities I could stomach and in turn showing me I could survive. Thank you for every example of what parents are not supposed to do so I never do them to my own children. Thank you for an education in ambivalence.

Thank you for the gift of never giving up.

When I think of Waterloo, I think of the tiny little victories I achieved as well. I pushed myself to self-educate and not just rely on the fast-food school system. When shit got to be too much, I wrote for days, or I read any book I could get my hands on, or I pushed myself to get out and find somewhere quiet, just to have some kind of sanctuary. I taught myself how to play guitar and drums. I wrote songs on the back of my homework assignments. When I tried to share them with others, they sneered and detracted from everything I wanted to be and accomplish. People will try to take anything they can away from you, especially when they think you have more than they do. Why is that almost always the case?

So maybe you are all "sinners." Maybe you deserve the filth that the religions of the world have smeared on your flesh. Maybe we are all just waiting to fry in Satan's Crock-Pot for the spiritual buildup that comes with too many hours left to your own devices. But what if you earn your sins? What if sins are like accolades? If sins are inevitable, and if that is the case, why fucking bother worrying about them in the first place?

All I know is what I have seen, and all I have seen is 98 percent of the world doing what they want. Think of it as the anthill being built out of the bodies the rogues never bothered to feed. Most do not care if they step on feelings, and the rest only care about their own feelings. Selfish hordes of useless boobs, desperately trying not to suck ass, scour the planet for a little piece of heaven before they shoot it all to hell. This is the world we leave behind. This is the world the saints died for. This is the world where I could not care less. Do I sound bitter yet? Yeah, I suppose I do. But you helped raise me, people, so suffer.

Waterloo, Iowa—an oasis of fuck in a world of shit and there are cities just like it all over the country, and if I had my way, I would use a bulldozer to pull every brick down, then I would pave the ground and leave a parking lot in its fucking wake. I would cleanse the earth to save its soul. It is a concrete cyst on an earthen scar that has been worried at by a half a million tongues until the area around it is chapped and useless.

There is a side of me that will always be the scared little coked-out misfit, stuck in a trailer and grasping at straws. There are nights I dream I am back there and I wake up screaming. There is a part of me that is very scared of the things I am capable of, and much like an addict, I dedicate myself to being better every day. I sin like crazy, but I protect my people. I work every second of my life and I do my very best to be the best father I can. All of this would not be possible if I had been raised in a psychological womb somewhere. I would not be *me* if I had not been *him* first, you know?

Radical change is a decision. You decide who or what you are going to be. If you are strong enough, you can dedicate your life to being exactly that. If you are not, you take the easy route— just going with the flow. People have told me sinning is easy but character takes work. I think it is as simple as this: People are easy and characters take practice. Sinning is just what most of us do when nobody is looking.

So I find myself right back at the place I was at in the first place: Sins are bullshit. They can build panache. They can spawn creativity. They can lead us to the truth. *They can set us free.* They can show us who we are, or who we want to be, if we just press our faces a little closer to the keyhole. What they cannot do is change anything at the end of the day. What are you going to do, dwell on it? Leave behind chances you could have taken advantage of because you think you do not deserve them?

This is either a great time for a story or a quote. I guess I will do both.

It was the summer of '88, and I had fallen in love. Her name was Jenny and she was the most beautiful girl I had ever seen, so much so that she is the face I used to compare every woman to, right up until recently. She had warm red hair and soft white skin, blue-green eyes and a sweet smell that was all her own. If she came in a room today, I could close my eyes and know she was there. She was the crush of a lifetime, the "almost was." I was a 25-cent rubber ball bouncing off of my own walls, red-eyed and blue-tailed, at war with everything around me. For some strange reason, she fell for me, too.

We were together for a summer, teenagers lost in the moment and each other's eyes. I wanted to spend every second with her—seriously. For some reason, when I was with her, I was not the kid who could not afford anything, could not take her anywhere, or could not give her anything. She brought peace and life into my world for a brief second, and then she took it away. She was young; fuck, I was young, too. That is all it was. That did not matter to me at the time. To me, time stopped when she let me go.

So do you know what I did? I did what any disrespecting man-boy would do in a similar situation. I dated her sister about four months later and I was the biggest fucking prick on the damn planet. I put that poor girl through hell. I was such a stool sample that her father rightfully threatened to kill me. I did this because I was a stupid kid who did not know any better. I did this because I wanted someone to hurt like I was hurting, and if I could not hurt the one I wanted to hurt, I would hurt her family. Why?

"Why": Where do you even start to answer that simple one-word quandary? As huge as our souls are purported to be, what fills us with a bigger satisfaction—love or revenge? Would we rather give it all or take it all? This quartz in our spirits has the capacity to break boundaries or hearts, and many people have done both, myself included. We are just the paperbacks of generations, left to be flipped through on an overcast afternoon, and how quickly we forget the twists at the end. Do we learn from past mistakes so we do not repeat them, or are we doomed to repeat them? If sin is the price for free will, what is the fucking point? Most of us never get to write the rules, so who are you to fucking judge me?

I have done shitty human things because I am human. It does not mean I am proud of it, but it also does not mean I brag about it, and it does not mean I forget. I am a man with a past, nothing more and, more importantly, nothing less. No one reads the future. If you are smart, you read the past to have better control of your present. We do what we can with the time we have. But it is our time nonetheless. At the end of the day it is the only thing that is truly ours. My time takes forever; hopefully yours does, too.

I have not seen Jenny or her sister in twenty years. There is a very good possibility that they do not even remember my sad Irish ass and that is fine. I can only hope the passage of time has dulled the pain I put them through. But I can still see the way their faces turned to stone the day they turned their backs on me. What price will you pay to have the satisfaction of seeing the ones who hurt you hurting as well? Spiritually, I would rather bounce that check in heaven then spend that money in hell. The ones you love usually bear the brunt of your highest highs and the lowest lows—the same goes for the ones you allegedly hate.

I know no one wants to hear about it, but there are human beings who bring out the best and, especially, the *worst* in us all. There is a chemical thing, a character thing, and we react whether we want to or not. So it comes to this: Assume sin exists. Now ask yourself if it is it a bigger sin to react horribly to someone you know will bring it out of you or to be the one who brings that out of anyone? People do not want to face that, but it is true. We all have emotional sonar, and we can hone in on the good shit, the bad shit, or the *really* horrible shit.

Anyway, it was a long time ago, but not so long, you know what I am saying? The rust does not buff out. Use all the Armor All you would like—you are who you are. Growing up in garbage is a lot like being a wise guy; you are in until the day you die. It will be with you for the rest of your life and the people you try to escape from will haunt you like Ebenezer Scrooge's ghosts on Christmas Eve. It is just like family: You choose your friends, but not your family. If they are south of outstanding, they will circle you like dead moons and pull you down into terminal gravity and tribulation. I do not say this with any malice. It is a fucking fact and it sucks, but survivors survive. You will always have one eye on the road and one on the rearview mirror.

As I am writing this, I am remembering more than I would like. My life has not been pretty. But I have not had it as bad as a lot of people have. And I am who I am today because of the positions I have been put in and the decisions I have made. If that means I am guilty forever, then so be it. But I am made to make: do not expect me to give a shit if it means I go against somebody else's book. Life is not that simple. That is why it is called *life*. That word includes both *lie* and *if*. Time to figure out which side of the "half" fence you are on: Does your *life* include a *lie* or just one big *if*? There is nothing wrong with either to be honest, but it will make your Sundays longer.

Here is a hot little piece of irrelevance that might interest you. Heat up some Pepsi and pull up a pillow, kids, Uncle Corey is going to scare the fuck out of you.

I was born December 8, 1973. At first glance, that does not seem all that interesting. But factor this in: Jim Morrison was born December 8, 1943, and died young. Sam Kinison was born December 8, 1953, and died young. Frank Sinatra Jr. was kidnapped on December 8, 1963. John Lennon was shot and killed on December 8, 1980. The night of December 8, 1984, was the night of the infamous Vince Neil car crash, in which Razzle, the drummer for Hanoi Rocks, was killed. I thought I was cursed.

So for the longest time, I was convinced I would be dead by the age of twenty-one. I had dreams about it all the time. I could never see a future past the flames of youth. Yeah, it sounds like bullshit, but at the time it was just what I knew. Now I am wondering if it was just the effects of too many years living in fuckland. I had to escape the pain of living to see what actual living was all about. So maybe I just thought I only had so much time to live and enjoy it. Man, was I stupid. You can only blame the ignorance of youth on being young because anyone old enough would know better, or at least have a fucking clue that something did not make sense.

My friend "Dimebag" Darrell Abbot was murdered on my birthday: December 8, 2004. I miss him a lot, especially with all the crap in music today. But I do not blame his death on some curse. I blame his death on the insane violence of a deranged human being. I blame his death on a random act, a selfish act that unfortunately left us with one less icon in a world short on originals. I remember that night, but most importantly, I remember the times I got to spend with my friend Dime.

So I learned to let go of youthful superstition and take life as it comes.

I am thirty-seven years old now and I am not so sure I know anything more than I knew yesterday, but I do know this: Life is better lived when you do not buy into what you think you know. It is better to know your way downhill than to try rolling up a mountain you have never seen before. Too many times I have dealt with mysteries beyond my control, and I have watched "geniuses" take a shot at figuring it out. Sometimes it is better to learn right along with everyone else than to assume you know shit about shit. A novice can rule the world; experts will get you killed every time. So what do I know? Not much, but more than most maybe. But at least I admit it. I have my share of answers, but I am still willing to learn. You can take a shower and still leave stains in your drawers. You can know a lot and still not know shit.

Why the fuck did I put this chapter in this book? Is it because of my sins, or other people's sins? Is it because of the monsters in my closet or the ones people have left in my house? I guess I want to tell everyone out there, all over the world, that no matter where you come from, it does not have to be who you are. It does not have to rule you. Your problems do not have to be someone else's problems. Humans are going to be who they are going to be and there is nothing you can do about it at the end of the day, but you can rise above all of it. You do not have to be a prisoner. You can be your own fucking hero. Am I ashamed of what I have done? Sometimes. Do I regret any of it? Depends. Would I do it all over again? Yes. I am not in *Star Trek*: I do not fuck with the space-time continuum, and I would not change who I am.

I think my trip down Nightmare Lane is just about over. Good riddance to mental clutter. I have talked about family and all the hell that follows with them. I have talked about life and all the hail and bullets that it brings to the poker table. I have talked about the consequence of regret and the little pings and pangs of glee that come from watching your enemies squirm around in their later, disposable lives. And I have not even come close to scratching the surface. There are still things I intend to keep a little closer to the chest because as bad as it is, I still feel the need to protect my family. There were laws broken. There was evidence burned, and there are nightmares, always the damn nightmares. But I wrote this chapter to prove a point, not to twist the rest of the book into some kind of ostentatious "check me out" autobiography. I am not writing my douche diary; I am expounding about sin and the shit it rode in on.

You want to know who you are? Figure it out for yourself. Do not let your surroundings dictate your identity. Do not let your parents or your families rule your sense of self. Do not let your past control your future. These things are entirely up to you and you alone. You make your own decisions. Strength will guide you. Weakness will allow you to hide behind shallow excuses. Sure, having a terrible childhood can be an easy way out of having to make good decisions. But there are also people in this world who grew up with so-called "normal" lives, and there are quite a few of them who are total dick stains. If you take shelter behind examples of why you do not have to assume responsibility for your actions, you will build a house in the darkness: alone, afraid, and prone to terrific flares of violent selfishness. That neighborhood will always be the backdrop for a myriad of terribly fantastic tragedies. Do yourself a favor and move out of your head.

In other words, if you want to be a son of a bitch, do not punk out and hide behind hang-ups. Just be a son of a bitch. In fact be the best son of a bitch you can be. Why not? At least you can be content and happy being shitty and miserable. Is that not what being human is all about? Is that not what living is all about? It must be, because apparently living outside the lines in contentment and fulfillment is a fucking sin. How fucking dare they? How dare they take a handful of completely natural impulses and make them fucking sins? Why? Are they themselves guilty of the sin of envy because we are guilty of being alive?

I will tell you one thing, if being a slave that haunted the city of Waterloo has taught me anything, it is this: The life you save may be your own, but the lives you fight for may save you in return. I would rather "waste" my time pointing out hypocrisies than give up on making people think. Sure, it looks easy and I look really good doing it, but it is tiring work that can only be achieved by imbibing gallons of black coffee, hundreds of cigarettes end over end, sugar, fat, and hours of terrible television. I do this for you—so suck it.

*   *

In the end I was an orphan with a huge family. I have been to war with myself and destroyed the other side, which leaves me wondering who really won those battles. I am a little bit of both and none of the above, an enigma who grew a mohawk into a mullet and back again, living to brag about both. The days and nights of posing caught a taxi with capricious youth but left their wallet at the club. I was one of many poster children who never cared less . . . until we realized they were our lives, too. Moonshine, smugness, and durability—this is the generation that that was angry enough to make a scene in the parking lot as well as the food court, but acerbic enough to smirk for their mug shots.

To romanticize my time in Waterloo would be to cheapen the shit I went through, but I am only who I am because of those experiences. The dichotomy of this really fucks with my head. I never want to go back there, but I remember every place I ever hung out there, every friend I ever had there, every trail, every house I ever lived in, every school I went to, every bus route, every girlfriend, every weekend blasted, every grade wasted, and every single minute I was there because at least I was alive. I may have been ravaged and I may still be fucked up about it, but I was alive. And when you can still recall every heartbeat, there has to be some good in that time—there *has* to be.

Where the wheels break spokes, the road is always a little ragged. That road only leads to heartache. Take an exit before you hit rock bottom. Find a nice place to pull off and get your shit together. Then, once you are back in the car, put on some music and keep driving. If you are lucky, you will leave that repressive place in your rearview mirror.

So my "sins" were born in a town with no more people than the biggest city in Rhode Island, and my soul saw the repercussions. But my iron remains forged in stronger stuff evidently, with a little ore here and there still unrefined. That is okay by me; the wonder is the wandering. I just wish my world were not so sad sometimes. But as sad as I get, as bundled into madness as I find myself at times, all I have to do is take a deep breath and remember that I am miles away from certain places. My depressing geographical map is still miles off, my GPS shows no blind spots, and I am still not back in Waterloo, Iowa, in 1984. My place is here, with my family, with my dreams, and with my sanity. Let the rest of the world go for all I care. I am going to be okay.

Sounds good. In fact, it sounds great.

Now, where was I?

I'm with Envy

"**W**hat the hell does that guy have? I have to have it!!"

"Ooh!! What the fuck is that? I have to have that!!!"

Envy: How much easier does it get, man?

Next to vanity, envy is probably the most basic sin on Mr. Blackwell's list. It is the critter in the crevices, the one just out of reach. It is the itch that scratches back. Come on, hands up, you know who you are—we are all envious. It is just really fucking easy to be envious of anything and anyone. It makes us angry, covetous, it can even turn us on, for what is lust but being envious and wanting someone's sex all over us. So if greed is the main ingredient in our sinful pie, envy is the secret spice that really pulls it all together. Along with the rest of our Deadly Seven, it has been around for a really long time. One of the Ten Commandments says "thou shalt not covet thy neighbor's wife." Apparently Ezekiel's wife was looking more like Rachel Hunter than Estelle Getty. So envy is nothing new. It is also nothing deadly.

Wanting something better—well, hell, that is the American Way, right? Envy puts hollow points in raw pulpy hope and leaves you armed with a life gun you can use to blow big holes in listlessness. And why not? If dreams are to be believed in this country, they are community property, a visceral birthright they hand out in the hospital with red, white, and blue pacifiers. All we need is a little raising so we know what to do with all that shiny freedom! Part of that rearing process is a healthy dose of envy. I do not know about you, but there's so much stuff I want and most of it resembles shit that someone already has. So why should I not want what someone else has? Just because it belongs to them, it does not mean more aren't being made in various sizes. Even if it is one of a kind, there is always some shithouse shack somewhere selling losers like me knockoff replicas that smell like cornmeal and melt in the rain.

Commercials are romantic comedies designed to make the consumer envious of the people and the product—the prettier the person, the more you really need those pants. Billboards look like subliminal messages, your own personal covetous strobe light if you drive fast like me, and their sole purpose is to dose you with fleeting glimpses of shit you do not have or have not seen. So you find yourself wanting shit you never knew you wanted. You become a Manchurian Candidate at Macy's, ready to walk away with the hand soap *and* the lotion. We are bombarded with things to covet at morning, noon, and midnight madness sales until it becomes commonplace. But that is my point: I do not believe envy is all that bad, and in this country or any other, how can you not feel envious? We are all made to feel inadequate and wanton from invisible promises in dark shadows; back-alley bliss can be yours if the avarice is right. We are outsmarted and outflanked by thoughts that are not even ours, and these motherfuckers expect us to be virtuous? Holy hog fucker, how do you say "eat my creamy asshole" in Latin?

Envy has its ugly mornings, but it can lead to ridiculous quirks as well. For instance, I have a weird fascination about what people keep in their refrigerators, especially in California. I do not know why. I will be at someone's house and I will find myself in the kitchen. Next thing you know the fridge door is wide open and I am bent over with my face buried deep inside its contents. Get your head out of the gutter—we already covered lust, you perverts. I have no clue what it is, but I am just curious to see what is in there. What is it about the way people group their produce or stack their lunchmeat or organize their beverages? I touch stuff, pick something up and put it back. I also smell everything. To me, a loaded fridge in the eight-one-eight is like a video game: I will jump right in and play whether I know what the plot is or not.

Then there are the people with lavish homes and expensive cars who like nothing in their iceboxes. These people are so wealthy that they eat out exclusively. So they deck out their rig with a few key items: mustard, half-jar of pickles, empty paper wrapper, stick of butter, and a box of Arm & Hammer baking soda in case both things go bad. What the hell? You almost have to try to be this eclectic. Poor people and college kids have this kind of shit in their fridges, not rich folk. I think it is a subliminal tactic to make people think they are less well off than they really are. By keeping a broke-ass refrigerator, you are hoping people will feel sorry for you. That is all well and good, but you cannot pull it off in Beverly Hills.

I am quite frankly one of the most envious people on the grounds right now. If envy really makes you green, I would be the Incredible Hulk ripping through Manhattan. I am competitive, brazen, pissed off, and scrambling for all I can get. So in my eyes, envy is not a sin because it is the gust of wind in my sails. I get three times as much done because I want to have everything available. Greed and envy are doing a little hoedown in my shit shack, and I am the auctioneer calling out moves and getting it done. But even I have limits when it comes to checking things off of the Craig's List in my soul. These days, people treat kudos and appreciation like fact and recitation. In a world so two-faced that it talks out of both sides of its mouth, awards and accolades have become a queer sort of compensation, and I for one am here to say it is bullshit.

Grammies, Emmys, Oscars, AMAs, Tonys, ESPYs—you know, people used to be able to feel good about stuff like this. But in the last few years, corruption has eroded the confidence of even the most ardent believers. People ask me all the time what it feels like to win a Grammy. I tell them I could not care less. Why should I give a shit about the Grammy awards? All you need to know about this farce you can find out by looking at the categories. There are shit tons of awards for pop, hip hop, country, and even Christian contemporary. Most times, some categories allow for genres to overlap. There are even several technical categories, and deservedly so. A lot of times the people in this industry forget who does the grunt work, so good for them. However . . .

There is *one* metal category. *One. Metal. Category.*

Winning the metal Grammy tends to make you feel like a healthy leper. Sure, you feel great for a second, but you are still fucked at the end of the day. One can make the argument that because there is only one metal award, by winning you are elite and even more special than all the rest. Then why even have as many categories as they do? The whole point is to feel special, to feel like you have accomplished something no one could in that moment. These days, the latest flash-in-the-pan wannabe, untalented hack stain will walk away with an armful of these glorified doorstops to the tune of praises sung by fake flattery. In an era when the very words we use are accused of being lies, what does that say about an award show aligned against half the competition? Besides, I do not put a lot of stock in awards. I put my stock in the commodity that keeps you where you are and blesses you with opportunities to practice what you preach. I put my stock in the fans because they are putting their faith in me. No other reciprocation could sound or taste as sweet.

Like lust, envy can get on top of you quick. All it takes is a glimpse or a passing fancy and you will be gripped by it. It will spoil your milk and sour your grapes. It will keep you on your side of the bed. You will chew the insides of your mouth at dinner. You will be a walking distraction in your own life. But when you can turn that envy into attainment, what could be a better feeling? I am not writing a prescription for instant gratification. The doctor knows better. What I am saying is that every once in a while a dream should come true. I am saying that envy is an effect and you can fill in the blank on the cause. We all fight for our tiny bit of the Boston Cream every second of every day. Why should we be denied little things when they could get us a long way? I think the time of feeling bad about the things we want should have come to an end a long time ago. We are evolving into fortune cookies, twisted and sweet, but the only message inside is guilt. Why even crack the seal on the plastic, man? What is the point of eating when all you get is force-fed a betting line of heartburn and heartache?

By now you may have the presumption that I am a blowhard troublemaker with a chip on my shoulder and a giant hole in my soul. That actually does not sound all that bad, really. One of my philosophies has always been, "if you do not say it, it does not get said." Basically saying, it means if you want something in life, speak up or shut up. I am saying we have enough to worry about in our lives without worrying how people who look nothing like anyone we should give a shit about feel when it comes to our decisions. There are days when the world should stay the fuck out of your business. Wanting something should not be a sin when everyone around is feeling the exact same fucking way. Being human is an instinct, not a source of religious scrutiny.

Nowhere does the concept have more impact than in the case of children. I can put it in this context: When I was a kid, all I wanted one Christmas was a set of Boba Fett Underoos. That was all I wanted. I ended up with an Atari 2600 and double-deck ghetto blaster. The disappointment I felt at the time was so crushing that I refused to speak to anyone for a week. A few months later I was being moved to Florida against my will and I had to leave behind all of my stuff. All of it. My ghetto blaster and my Atari 2600 were pawned for gas money. I ended up homeless for a few weeks in Fort Lauderdale. By then, Boba Fett Underoos were the least of my worries. Eating had become a high priority. So I learned young that envy is silly in comparison with survival. It does not mean I stopped wanting my heart's desires. It means I have a curious yet headstrong way of putting things in perspective. I can see the forest through the fire. We make mountains out of gravel and ado out of apathy all the time. Envy will always be the Iago to our Othello.

Here is another bit of nonsense I came up with when I was younger. I was convinced I would never be a good singer or a great writer because I was not Steven Tyler. True story: Steven Tyler is one of the most gifted and original rock stars on the planet. Nobody sounds like him, nobody writes like him, and nobody exudes the kind of cool he has radiated consistently since I was a fucking toddler. He may have had his problems and he may go to battle with demons on a daily basis, but to me he was the upper crust of amazing. I have my idols: Sebastian Bach, Henry Rollins, Mike Patton, James Hetfield, and David Lee Roth. But Steven Tyler was the Holy Grail to me. He was the icon I tried to live up to for years.

As I got older I realized that I could never be Steven Tyler nor should I want to be, not because I think any less of him but because I know in my heart that emulation is a sincere form of flattery, but individuality is the only form of immortality. As envious as I was of his career, to want to have an exact replica would be a testimony to his legacy, not mine. It is easier to take your cues from someone else because they have made the mistakes in advance. No risk means no foul, but it also means no glory. You have to cut a new swath to find new land. If you follow the same path everyone else does, you will only end up with everyone else. If you want to stand out, stand up for yourself. So my loud envy became quiet respect for the Toxic Twin with the amazing lips. I still think he is an incredible man, but now I am looking for a way to be an equal not a double. Maybe that still means I am envious of a status high above what I have achieved. Maybe I am pragmatic and I know I have been extremely lucky to have the career I have had so far.

I am not the first to desire some sort of recognition from my elders. We have always envied the ones before us, whether it is a teenager wanting to be treated like an adult or a worker wanting a little respect from the boss. We all want the top spot, no matter where that spot happens to be. It can be as normal as walking through your neighbor's house with an eye for what you can improve in your own. It can be as sordid as an oedipal complex and a cocked fist. We fight the good fight, but when no one is looking, we will always find ourselves looking around. Envy will make a man cheat on his wife. Envy will make a wife fuck the pool boy. Envy will make us all fuck each other over to get a better washer and dryer. But is it a sin or is it one of those things that come standard like a GPS in a Lexus?

The devout masses have told us time and again that free will was a gift from God. I dread to say it but that makes my point. Free will is the box set and your "sins" are the DVDs. We come loaded with the propensity to do great and terrible things. Free will guarantees we can do them. But then we are expected to believe that someone is watching everything we do and judging every second. Why the fuck do we have free will if we are judged regardless? And why should we give a rat's ass pipe if we are being judged in the first place if we all have free wills? I guess it all comes down to what you believe. If you are an atheist, you just have to deal with how other people view your deeds. If you are a member of the holy flock, not only do you have to put up with the rest of the Gladys Kravitzes of the world, but you also have to worry about the big scary old guy in the sky. Your only hope is to subscribe to the New Testament god. He is a little more lenient than the Old Testament god. New Testament god will shake his head with a quiet knowing smile. Old Testament god will make you eat your children just to prove to him that you believe in his existence.

My own observations have shown me that envy just makes a sadistic little sewing circle that complains about anyone not knitting their ass off. For some reason we cannot keep our noses to ourselves. If we all just took life at face value, it might be a little easier. But most people just refuse to see that some things are unattainable. I get it: Every guy wants a four wheeler and every woman wants a guy who does not want a four wheeler. If people would just lower their expectations, they could settle, you know, like people do already whether they realize it or not. We get what we get and we like it, even if we do not truly like it. That is one thing about envy that I cannot stand: It makes us hate the things we get because they are not the things we want. Why do we not want the things we get? I am certain there are others who get the same shit. But we do not pay attention to those people. The things we get cannot be all that great because *those* people have them. So envy gives us another reason to look down on those around us, even when we are secretly looking up to them.

I will tell you what I do not envy. People with athlete's foot are nothing to be jealous of. Another example is the life of a garbage disposal. That is just gross. How about the snot end of a diseased penis? Where am I going with this? Sorry, I am surrounded by people talking about stuff I am actually interested in. I will be right back.

*   *

Okay, it is a day later and I have coffee, quiet, and countenance. Living with a million people in several different households makes it difficult to concentrate. Mornings like this make me envy a writer in his wood-ensconced study, complete with fireplace and loyal golden retriever. I have a kitchen table, a rotating space heater, and an ashtray covered in skulls wearing giant headphones. If you try sometimes, you just might find you get what you need. Thank you, Mr. Jagger.

There is a moment in everyone's life when you find yourself coveting something better, something meaningful, and something of merit. Dan Marino was one of the greatest quarterbacks of all time and yet he never won a Super Bowl. I will bet you a ton of money that he envies Trent Dilfer, who won a Super Bowl with the Baltimore Ravens. The Rock and Roll Hall of Fame is loaded with people who may or may not deserve to be there. How do you think that makes bands like Kiss and Rush feel, who are two of the most influential bands of all time who are still not in the Hall of Fame? People can go on and on about how they are content with what life has given them. But at night, when they are alone and the only voice asking them questions is in their head, the truth hangs in the silence like a heavy fog on the moors. I believe we are never truly content, but I think most of us can come close. It all depends on the details. I am a man with a deep hole inside me that I have tried to fill with all manner of subterfuge. I will not be a man satisfied until I am a man exhausted. We are given dreams so we can imagine a life that is a little more vested in the future. We are given life so we can exist. Our minds are what stoke the embers of desire. If God had wanted us to live without "sin," he should have never given us the power to think for ourselves.

That is truly the crux of my argument: People have developed into beings that would give anything to be free. We have seen it in revolution after revolution: men and women banding together to shuffle off an immoral coil disguised as a government that does nothing but everything of, for, and by themselves. The crooked claw their way into the hearts of leadership to dismantle and control the very tools we were given to live our lives. The further we get from the prologue, the closer we get to the exciting conclusion. This is in the spirit of the great minds who have tried to pull us together for something we never even knew we deserved. I am doing my best to carry on that tradition, to convince the people to rise up and tell the ones writing the rules that we will not be cabled into one universal rule of thumb. I am trying to set us free, but just with a few more fart jokes than you are probably used to.

In a world where the infirm are minutes away from walking on their own and the guilty are finally coming to justice even several years later, we are taking shaky steps toward letting go of myth and superstition and accepting ourselves for who we are: imperfect creatures of chance. Paint your Easter egg any color you want—we were accidents of evolution. We are a combination of aberrant cell growth, electrical synapse activity, and unbelievable luck. We are what happens when smart monkeys fuck. Making it more than it ever was just confuses the ignorant and slows our advancement. I am probably offending a lot of you, but I do not care. We should be looking inside for answers, not digging in the dirt to find ancient texts that supply a backstory. The future is meant for those who are willing to let go of the worst parts of the past. When you cannot take two steps without turning around to inspect your footsteps, you are getting nowhere fast. I know my ancestors blazed a trail somewhere around my family tree. So I will keep my eyes on the road, my hands on the wheel, and my ears open for distress calls.

Envy is not only limited to awards and flattery; it can also come in a form of jealousy that is as common as a fart after broccoli (see?). I call it the Married Man Melancholy. This comes when a married man is afflicted with a malady so viral it threatens the very fabric of his matrimony. It stings the heart, pierces the harmony, and leaves you going over your choices in life like unpaid bills at tax time. I am talking, of course, about single friends, but I do not mean the standard-issue, factory-built single friend who is looking for love but remains forlorn, watching *You've Got Mail* all alone on a Friday night. I am in fact talking about the single friend who lives like Hugh Hefner in the '60s and then tells you all about it later on. To your wife, he is known as the Best Man at your wedding and that Fucking Friend of Yours every day after your wedding. And he will drive you to cry in your Frosted Flakes a lot.

This single friend cannot wait to share his sexual exploits with you, sometimes calling you in the middle of the night while he is still at the woman's house. This single friend has gestures and hand signals that would make a deaf person call the police. This single person probably has a collection of soiled underwear in a "trophy case" somewhere in his closet, taking them out on Wednesdays to "count his scalps" when nothing is good on TV. This single friend is a scumbag, a total asshole, and a mangy dog of another color. You secretly love him for it.

The married man will live vicariously through his single friends when married life is starting to taste like warm water. I know, marriage is about the long term and a deeper love that lasts well after the romance is gone. But a man is also a creature of instinct if not habit, and he never misses a chance to take a look at another woman. It does not mean he is going to run out and shove his fuck pump into the nearest and most welcome vagina—it just means that he is looking. Women cannot handle it, and it causes a lot of bullshit. But this is just how guys are. We are mammals with a nose for pheromones, the great truffle hunters searching for the quickening and trying desperately to hide our massive hard-ons. Because of this, we carry a garbage truck–sized amount of guilt with us from day one to judgment day. It is not our fault; we go where the wind takes us. But the sanctity of wedlock holds a tight tether, leaving us to fight these feelings to keep our wives happy, our days less chaotic, and our homes quiet.

But it does not mean we cannot live another life through our friends. This is envy in its most pure and unrefined form. It gives us something to think about while we toil in cubicles or pound out manual labor. It gives us just a little hint of spice in our diets. Sure, we know it is just a flight of fancy, but inside we can transcend the bland and be a little less cramped if only for the briefest of periods. I do not say this to make people think that marriage is a burden; I am saying this is really just how guys are. Bad marriages are burdens and good marriages are godsends, but men will always just be men. Women, however, envy wholly different things. Not being a woman myself, mind you, this is just speculation, but I think I have a pretty decent grasp on this. Women do not envy silly things like dirty sex or drunken fiascos, although I am sure they enjoy both when readily available. No, women envy the things that truly matter in the world: status and stability.

A woman will live above her means to appear wealthier, more glamorous, and more confident than she really is her whole life. She will scramble and scrape for every little piece of the good life she can muster to get ahead and stay there. You may think this is a selfish little bit on her part, and on mine for writing it. But I disagree for one big reason: Men have done so much to ensure that women remain behind them that the ladies have had to adapt this reflex. Since the invention of talking, women were delegated to keeping the house and appearances for the caveman provider, thus beginning a millennium of competition between the sexes that crested with Susan B. Anthony and culminated with the Equal Rights Amendment. I know and you know that women are just as good and fucked up as men. In the end they will win their rights.

But in the back of their cerebrals, there was that instinctual tickle that craved status and hungered for not only a seat at the table but also the nicest most expensive table on the cul-de-sac. Much like the inner battle that men face every day keeping the sexual seed spreader at bay, women fight their own secret Gettysburg trying to balance a world where they have the right to be whatever they choose and yet still are worried about what the neighbor's house is worth. I am guaranteed a verbal bitch slap for saying this shit, but the truth is a sledgehammer. I am just the guy in the hard hat swinging it. I see it every day because I work with several strong, committed women who are almost always better than the men they work for. I have had the privilege of picking the brains of quite a few females in a position of power far above mine. They are vital, sharp instruments of intelligence and savvy and they know exactly what they want. But every fucking time, what they want is usually what somebody else has. So women are not immune to the allure or the palpable thrust of envy. They just envy different things. Some would say better things. I would say more esoteric things.

But the price of longing is charged to a credit card that does have limits. There is a finite reservoir we carry around like a camel hump. If you get what you want all the time, you will end up with all the time you want and nothing to show for it. There is a certain candor that comes with denying satisfaction. It builds character, breeds appreciation, and allows for achievements of real worth. Yeah, you get pissed for a while, but who really needs a bidet in their garage? Come on, we have to start being practical with our envious whims. This is a country that does not like being practical, though. This is a country of game shows and instant winners, of self-starters and risk takers. This is a country where everything can be yours if the price is right. So common sense does not really blend when all-out instinct goes into the game plan. People will fill out Publisher's Clearing House entries until their eyes go numb in the hopes that they can win $10 million in forty-eight hours. Then they will not have to watch MTV's *Cribs*—they can be on it. Never mind the fact that *Cribs* features the homes of the famous. When they win their money, they *will* be famous. Never mind the fact that most of the bragging, grinning cocksuckers on *Cribs* do not even own the houses they are showing off. It does not matter. As soon as they get something for nothing, all their troubles will go away.

There you go, people. As soon as you get something for nothing, all your troubles will go away. Is that true? Is it just that simple? It seems to me that the people who play these games were not all that great with money to begin with, so what the fuck are they going to do with $10 million? They will wipe their ass with it. Then they are back at square one, with debt and interest. Good luck fishing that golden hook out of your sphincter: It has a barbed end and leaves a mark like a fucker. Use your pinky, it just might help. But common sense logged out of our chat rooms right around the time Thomas Paine died. It fled the scene like last call at a strip club, leaving us with soiled bills and creepy uncles lounging around sniffer's row. The American Conversation has become a monosyllabic, incoherent mess of dudes, bros, fucks, and Lindsay Lohan. All we care to talk about are things we cannot have, people we cannot be, and places we cannot go. In other words, the American Conversation is a fucking love story devoted to envy. And why not, man? We preach a new religion, so why should we not have the best god money can buy? We show the best shows and move the best moves and just out and out outdo the rest of this giant blue pimple of a planet. Why not rub it into the global eyeballs a little further? If plights are the wounds this world tries to live with, America is a fucking ten-year-old with a Super Soaker full of lemon juice and dog piss. I think this is one of the reasons we go to war every ten years. We get really mad if we find that a country does not have the decency to envy our freedom like the rest of the world does. If we cannot be the most popular kid in school, we will burn the cafeteria to the ground. Do not pass go. Do not collect $200. "Exterminate all the brutes!" Makes you want to salute a flag right now, huh? I am confident that is exactly what our founding fathers were trying to accomplish when they set down the blueprints for our timeless civil liberties. I love being American, but I hate other Americans.

So you see, this feeling of envy permeates us all. I am sure most of you would be very upset if I accused you of being dirty, stinky sinners, almost as sure as I am that you are all dirty, stinky sinners, but not because of envy. We all fight off bouts of boring inner botulism that threaten the sweetbreads of our soul, but wanting more and wanting it better than before is no reason to throw out last night's chicken yet. It makes no difference to me how you feel, really. I know where my moral limits lie. Envy comes with the territory, and if you want to lose sleep over shit you cannot control, go right ahead. Sorry, I have an allergy to stupidity. So I spend a lot of time sneezing, especially in airports. I go through tons of Kleenex. That is why I am angry with you people. You make me sneeze. *Stop being stupid!*

You would not bother me so much if you were not so envious of idiotic tool bags like Nicole Richie and Tila Tequila. These people make armpit farts seem classy. They are sprayed all over TMZ and *Us Weekly* like cold jizz in a public bathroom. They are hardly glamorous, have no fucking talent whatsoever, and serve no real purpose other than to make us feel bad about not being them. They remind me a lot of the dried remnants of rogue piss that collects and creates the orange crust around the bolts on a bachelor's toilet: As soon as you find yourself with that problem, you have made a filthy mess and it is going to take a long time to come clean. There are genuine superstars in this world that could not give a dried deer turd whether or not they are in *People* or the *Enquirer*. I am still trying to figure out who in the hell this Heidi Montag person is and why I should give a red shit or even why I know her damn name. Apparently she is a singer. Apparently she got fucking married. And apparently all you people cared. I still do not have the faintest clue. I know she is blonde (until it is no longer stylish), I know she has a mouth a train could drive through, and I know without a shadow of a doubt that I do not find her appealing in the slightest. I do not envy her life at all. But some of you do. Why would you envy anyone who looks like a stunt double at the Preakness?

Is it the money? You can make money, kids. Even people living on the street make money. That is not that difficult. Hell, I knew a dude named Smiley who did nothing but collect bottles and cans and bum spare change from the moment he woke until the moment he finally slept. He had a fucking house *and* a high-end Lexus. So do you envy the money? Do you think if you are famous you are automatically wealthy? Nothing could be further from the truth. I am slightly more famous than most and I make a decent living in my tax bracket, but I am far from wealthy. I cannot yet buy the things I want to buy. But once I am incredibly rich, I will have these things, like an island, a houseboat, another island . . . and Wyoming. But I am still famous. Several of you reading this book know who I am. Some of you might think I am the gay porn star Corey Taylor. I am deeply flattered! But no . . .

By the same token, is it the fame? Do you envy them for their relative notoriety? Do you wish you could walk into a restaurant and get a table immediately, even if you still have to pay full price? That is not a very good reason either. First of all, most famous people are secretly angry about being famous. They do not like being bothered just because you recognize who they are, even though they would be hotter under the designer collar if you did not recognize them. Yeah, they hate being famous, until they are not famous anymore. Then they just hate you. Having said that, I have to tell you fame is not all it is cracked up to be. I am the kind of guy who is still surprised when anyone recognizes me, but there are definitely times when it sucks, like walking through the mall when you have to piss really bad, knowing there are five or six thirteen-year-olds following your every move. You feel like you have been tagged by *National Geographic*.

So what is it you envy about these scags? Do you envy their looks? Jesus, Howard, Fine, Howard, and Christ, some of these people look misshapen. Others look like skeletons. The rest are too weird to really get a bead on. There is that guy from the Twilight movies who looks like Count Chocula had a baby with Frankenberry. There is Ashlee Simpson—oh, excuse me, Ashlee Simpson-Wentz. She looks like a cross between a chipmunk and a rat attack. There is the "basic hot" brigade, people like Jessica Simpson and Gwen Stefani. Why do you envy them—because a couple of fucking cheerleaders did something other than wind up working at Hooters? We have stopped giving adulation to the truly talented and started giving it to the truly average in the hope that by lowering the bar, we ourselves might be eligible for the fame and glory. Maybe that is why all we do is clamor and cling to their coattails and cuffs. We might just be them some day.

Hell, it may not be that far off. *American Idol* does huge numbers in the first few weeks and the last few weeks, which means two things: We all want to see the winners in the end but we also want to scoff at and enjoy the losers who get ripped to shreds in the beginning. I have seriously never seen an episode of *American Idol* past the first two shows of every season. It is sadism at its greatest: the pointing and the laughing as, one by one, these brave and cocksure hopefuls make and snake their way around a line that might as well get them into Disneyland, waiting hours and hours for a thirty-second chance to maybe make it onto the next half of the show. What they show you is a condensed version with lots of highlights you can chuckle and feel good about, because if you think about it too long, you will realize you are a fucking asshole for doing so. What they do not show you are the hours these people spent waiting and how they got more and more nervous and probably threw up a couple different times. Here is some perspective: The same people who laughed at William Hung most likely bought his fucking album. So sit in that shit.

If sins were a Broadway play, these seven would play out as such. Anger would be the high-energy, high-stepping opening number. Vanity would be the duet between the leading stars, all in spotlight with no one else on stage. Lust would be the "orgy" number. Greed would be the solo number for the villain. Gluttony would feature way too much dancing. Sloth would be another boring ballad. All of this would have a lot of red and black-light spots shining, velvet curtains flying around from the jet engine fans blowing shit all over, and glittery staircases that are a little too high and lead nowhere. The songs would seem a little risqué, the dancer would show a little too much pussy and cock, and the marquee names attached to the project would be the musical equivalent of Spam and nutmeg.

Envy's number would be the only shining star in the show, because it would go completely over people's heads. It would have to be the duet between the villain and the hero, but it would slowly morph into an ensemble piece that involves everyone and it would have to be written in such a way that you would not know who was who because both the villain and the hero suffer the "sin" of envy. The villain envies the hero because he gets the girl. The hero envies the villain because the villain does whatever he wants. The girl envies the villain because he gets to be bad. The chorus line envies the core cast because they get their names on the playbill. The dancers envy the chorus line because they do more than just dance. Meanwhile the audience envies everyone on the stage because they are in a Broadway show. So envy would have to be the closing number because it would be the one theme that ties us all together at the end of the night. That is the time of the day when envy hits you where you live. We all go back to where we came from, and the whole time we are wondering what everyone else is doing, envying the mystery of their exploits. It is no mystery; our fantasies are always greater than the sum of all their realities. But we still pine for their lives while next door your neighbor pines for yours, and so on and so on.

We all do it. We all feel it. We all deal with it. It is a tie that binds all different kinds. So here is my question: If this is a concept that we all experience and we all let bring out the best and worst in ourselves, how can it be a sin? Remember: Sin equals bad, and if you are a sinner, you are a bad person. So are you? Do you consider yourself a person of ill intent? Here is something to think about: A villain is nothing more than someone who is convinced that he or she is right. We have always been two halves making one whole. We have both dark and light sides. Anyone who has an eye and a handle on both is just a little further ahead than the rest of us. And that is someone I envy most of all.

Greedy Little Pigs

Mmmmmm . . . . Greed. Sweet, indulgent, creamy greed: more, more, more for me, *Me, ME*. It is as benign as season tickets and as intricate as a Ponzi scheme. It has driven men and women to commit horrendous acts of selfish atrocity, like crushing one another in a mall, scrounging for Cabbage Patch Kids, Beanie Babies, or the latest PlayStation. In short, it can and will make you insane. Sadly, it is not like Christmas: It comes more than once a year and no one is greedy for socks, except Wembly from *Fraggle Rock*, who does not count because he is a puppet and, therefore, not real. Then again it could have been Gobo; I get all my puppets mixed up sometimes.

Greed is the urge to own and obtain every action figure on the planet. Greed is the needle in the back of your neck that pushes you to add extra zeroes to your own bankroll check at the office. Greed is the never-ending search for a completion of self that, sadly, may never come. It is in all of us, and it is inevitable. It is wealth and stuff and class and holdings and everything else that spins the head from time to time. There is a very serious problem with greed at the moment, but we will get to that later. Let's do some background and figure this out before we go any further, shall we?

Greed is a very special sin on this list because in a lot of ways, without greed, some of the other sins would not exist. Think about envy—what is envy but being so greedy you want someone else's shit? Gluttony is just greed for a particular thing, be it food or otherwise. Lust is an all-consuming greed for sex at all times; even vanity is a sort of greed for the flesh, wanting only to be the most beautiful creature known to man and Ted Koppel. Without the others, greed could stand on its own, a self-fulfilling sensation. But without greed, a lot of these supposed sins could not get off the runway.

Maybe that is the reason it comes first on so many lists of the deadly sins. It is certainly the most powerful and yet it is the most esoteric. It is not pure emotion like anger; it is not a physical rapture like lust. It is not easily recognized like sloth or vanity. But greed, when not kept in check, can warp the very Oak of Man more crookedly than all the waters of the world.

So, having said that, *I am a greedy fuck.*

I want it *all*, and I have no qualms about admitting or even embracing it. I want to have more money than God. I want to do every little thing that comes to mind. I want to write and star in a major motion picture. I want to be the biggest-selling musical artist of all time. I want to own land and have cool shit like compounds and nightclubs. I want to be feared and revered because of power and excellence. Shit, even writing this book is an example of my greed; sure, it has been a dream since I was a kid, but I am greedy enough to want to be successful at it. So it comes down to semantics, where one man's greed is another man's ambition, and I have never seen ambition on a sin list yet.

I understand the consequences of being driven into the ground by this acumen. But I also know that greed has another side to its coin. Greed can push people to be and do their utmost best, ultimately achieving success and renown for ingenuity and innovation. It can cause a revolution; it could cure cancer. It can bring us screaming into the millennium with advances and hurtling toward the sunshine with breakthroughs. It can open the flood gates to a host of different ways we can all get ahead in this crazy, kooky Jetsons world we are living in right now.

All because some guy wants the money that the patents will bring in.

Nothing wrong with that, people, nothing at all wrong with that. It takes something special to get us humans off of our asses and disengaged from episodes of *House* long enough to heal the world, and I am here to tell you that it is not always charity and good will. Sometimes the only reason to show up to the award show is the fucking goodies bag, you see the metaphor? Now granted, some people work tirelessly to effect change in this world purely for the joy of bringing light into the very darkness that barks at our doorsteps. But somewhere, deep down, a lot of them want something. Most of us, I posit, are spurred on by a vicious little vibe called the Urge.

The Urge is the voice in all of us that has a bottomless pit for a soul and all the free time it could ever need. It feeds on the longings we try to keep quiet and it bolsters the mindset that cannot live without our heart's desires. It is located right next to your cerebral cortex, lying in wait for those opportune moments when it can spring into action and sell the brain on a simple little tagline:

More, more, more for me, *Me, ME* . . .

But does this make it a sin? Does this make it deadly? I do not believe so. In fact, the more I think about it, the more I am assured that this sin in particular makes my point. We are all greedy in some way. We do not all subscribe to the same neo-Christian doctrines, and yet we all feel the brunt of the same human traits. So if being greedy is just another way of being human, then the righteous are saying that being human is a sin. I dare them to say that shit to my face.

I have a really great argument against "greed is a sin" dog shit. Have you ever eaten one single M&M? Hmm? Have you ever used just one single square of toilet paper? Have you ever limited yourself to just one ketchup packet? Have you ever slept more than your allotted government-recommended eight hours a night? Well, not only have you been a glutton and a sloth (allegedly), you have been greedy.

On behalf of my fellow M&M lovers everywhere, I would like everyone who thinks like that to kindly go fuck themselves. Greed is just the genetic need to acquire, and that has been going on since we moved into frickin' caves: "We need grass on the floor, and it *has* to match the moss on the walls." We are hunter/gatherers, and if you did not bring back the bigger brontosaurus, you had to go club your neighbor to death and take his.

Leave it to religion to make greed a sin, by the way. I know how it started. In its heyday (i.e., the Middle Ages), the Church was not only the seat of spiritual mercy and grandeur but also the place to obtain an education. Colleges were built by the clergy and, more importantly, *for* the clergy. In order to attend, you had to become a priest. Most commerce was presented within spitting distance from the Church's doorstep, and usually the vicars got a little kickback for their trouble. So imagine its dismay if someone came along who was wealthy and a little bit ahead of the curve in the smarts department—Q.E.D.: "He or she is guilty of the sin of greed!"

What a crock. Was the Church not greedy when they kept education for themselves? More to the point, are religions not guilty of greed and vanity when they say their "god" is the only real god and their teachings are the only real teachings, and they try to hoard all the followers by decrying the other side? It is horseshit; any religion that preaches one-sided doctrines is not religion at all but a fucking recipe for control and hate. I am talking about Christianity, Islam, and any other way of life that tries to control life itself. The zealots of the world are using faith as a race to see who can sell the most holy cookies because whoever has the most followers wins. They combine scripture and conspiracy theory to fashion a mandate that will attract the human flies to the sticky trap. We are the equivalent of religious capital—nothing more. When those who are leading the masses are doing so not because they are teaching but because they are obsessed about winning, you can see that greed can corrupt the most ardent and proves that no one is above reproach. We are human: We are flawed, and saying that some people are not culpable is blasphemous to the human condition.

*   *

On a lighter note, I love movies!

I have several thousand DVDs in a room I call the Vault. It is air conditioned to maintain the proper temperature because my comic books are also in there. The movies are alphabetized, followed by any titles that start with a number. The room has several shelves that encircle its circumference. It now has a lock on the door because my friends borrow movies and never bring them back. Hey, fuckface, I'm not Blockbuster. I will break your fucking hands and legs. Bring back my copy of *I Spit on Your Grave*, Mike!

I have so many movies that many are still in the plastic. I have so many movies that I forget what movies I have and I rebuy them and end up giving the old ones away. I have so many movies that I sometimes keep the multiple copies because there are different versions. I have around twelve different versions of *Reservoir Dogs*: I have the regular one, all the different colored tenth anniversary editions, the special edition Gas Can package that was released for the fifteenth anniversary, and the Blu-ray version. If I am anything, I am a collector and an enthusiast. But here is my question: What is the difference between greed and collecting? Where does fandom end and fanaticism begin? Is it greed if all my movies are alphabetized?

We are all guilty of some greed. Think about those times when you need a penny at the convenience store, and you know you have a penny in the pocket of your skinny jeans and you take one from the penny plate anyway. Think about those times you were strolling through the grocery store and you took a few pieces from the Brach's candy display. You guys do remember Brach's candy, right? No? *Fraggle Rock* neither? Damn, I am getting old.

You can call it stealing, but I call it greed. You did not need that penny or that delicious candied root beer barrel, but you took it anyway. You wanted to have it so no one else could. That makes you a bad person. Not really, but it does make you human. We all want not only our fair share but whatever is left in the till as well. It is like eating all the fries at the bottom of the bag when you know some of them were in your wife's order of fries as well. The whole human race is trying desperately to get more for their money, the spiritual super-saver deal so to speak. Is that greed? Not necessarily. You do not have to be greedy to stand in line for a discount. But the base measure of wanting and needing is in that very concept of necessity. Bring a man a glass of water and he will drink it, no questions asked. Bring a man a shot of whiskey and he will complain over whether it is scotch or bourbon. Personally, I prefer rye, but that is just me.

A lot of people are going to say this book is just a way for us all to get away with proverbial murder, but my point is much simpler. We all carry so much fucking baggage in our lives that the last thing we need is more shit we do not need from people we do not know. It is like when you see the sequel to a movie you love—you already know what has happened beforehand. The backstory goes without saying. So if we all know we are human and we are going to make mistakes, why keep shoving it down our throats? Do you want us to choke on morality or spit resentment into your pupils? We know we are flawed. We learn from flaws. Our flaws make us unique. We are the soiled snowflakes of history. But to say we are going to burn in your hell not only for being born but also for being alive is the greatest piece of hypocrisy ever committed to myth. The cocksuckers that be will forever try to put the "wrong" in your right to be anything, and they are terrified that someone is going to come along and call them on their bullshit. That time is now; that someone is me.

Reality is notorious for putting its own unique spin on the status quo. There is a common misconception among the believers and the shakers that damnation lies in laying down with evil in its most dubious form. However, the truth is far from where they stand. The devils we know do not come in any medieval or fantastic guise—no red suits or pitchforks, no fire or brimstone. They look like you and me. The devil you have to watch out for looks like your neighbor, talks like a salesman, and feels like your best friend. Holy help you if you get all three.

*   *

Here is a tawdry little tale for you. About ten years ago I was taught a very valuable lesson about greed. I had just received a sizable check, or as I am prone to call it, "coin of the realm," because you never know when you are going to find it. Anyway, I received this check and I thought my life was signed, sealed, and delivered from evil. I had never made that much money in my entire life; in fact, if you were to add up all the money I had ever made in my life up until that point, it would not have equaled this one check. I am not bragging; if I were, I would tell you the amount. It was not in the millions or anything. I am just putting it into perspective so you understand what happens in the rest of this story. People say money does not buy you happiness. What they do not tell you is that losing money will make you lose your mind.

Anyway, I fell into the same cliché mistake that I had always read about. After I had spent a bunch of it, I decided I was going to "play it safe" and invest it into companies that I would either start myself or that already existed. So the first company I invested in was a T-shirt company that I had been planning to start with a person I will call Jimmy. Jimmy and I had been talking about doing something together for a long time, and it seemed that now that I had the capital to do so, we could get started. We decided to start simple and print white-on-black T-shirts with clever sayings that we had come up with. It was fool-proof—no artwork to reproduce and no writers to pay off. So I sent Jimmy a large deposit of money to get things started. I know what you are thinking and I concur. That was indeed my first mistake. Do you know what Jimmy did? He used some of the money to print a few T-shirts that he then let sit in boxes and he spent the rest because it was a business expense, that is, he did not have a job and he needed gas, food, and cigarettes. After going back and forth with Jimmy for several months, I finally cut ties with him and wrote off the money as a loss. It was not like I was going to make the same mistake twice, right?

So the second mistake I made was a tattoo shop I helped start with a friend I will call Louie. Louie was a really good tattoo artist and had already started one shop in town with someone else. He was looking to start his own and I was looking for some way to get some money back and still be a sort of loud silent partner. So a plan was hatched: Find a spot where there would be little competition in our field and not only offer tattoos but also piercing, T-shirts, and jewelry. I advanced him a good chunk of change and, while I was at it, bought some ad time at some of the local radio stations for good measure. It was only a matter of time before I would see a little return on my invest-ment. You have to love the indestructibility of youth.

The shop, as you can guess, was a flop. Louie set it up an hour outside of Des Moines in a town that suffered from chronic small town hypocrisy. He also hired two of the worst artists in the business to help him. The place was churning out shitty ink at high prices. I tried to buy more ad time to get more business, but it was no use. The shop went under. Louie went off and started another shop with another sucker. I ate another handful of shit to go with the money I had lost. It was okay, though. It was not like I was going to make the same mistake three times, right?

So the third mistake I made was the worst of all. It involved people who were very close to me and it rips my heart to pieces to think about it. Out of respect to them, I will keep their identities completely anonymous. It makes no difference, though. The loan was substantial. The loss was incredible. I literally have nothing to show for it. I have not been the same since. I ended up in financial trouble, and for a few years I was chasing the tail end of a tax debt I had not planned to have. Greed had made me think I was smarter than I really was with money. If I had sat on that money, I would be doing very well right now. Instead I turned into some kind of carpet-bagging lunatic trying to triple every cent in my pocket. If the whole ordeal taught me anything, it is this: Greed makes you do the most inconsiderate shit on the planet . . . and I should have just stuck to singing.

I recovered from my follies, thank god. I never got a dime back from any of them, but I can say karma is a toothy rabid dog. Jimmy is now broke and his teeth have rotted out of his face. Louie lost everything, including his wife, and had to leave town. The other people, well, let's just say they are living in a hell I would not even want to drive by on a road trip. In the end, the experience and the knowledge I took away from it all has been wonderful. Today I am smarter with my money and let people who do it professionally handle it for a modest fee. I do not start or invest in companies anymore: I buy houses. Real estate may fluctuate, but everyone needs a house at some point. I set up college funds for my children and I am saving the rest for a houseboat. That way, no matter where I am floating, that is where I live. The way was rough, but I got there. I am wiser than I have ever been. I am not a genius—I still forget to put the seat down and my wife hates it. But I am getting there. So after all the things I have taken away from that and all the things I have learned, I can safely say that without greed I would not have become the man punching these shiny keys today. If I took so much away because of greed, how can that be a sin?

People get uncomfortable wanting things. It makes them feel like Peter Lorre in *M*. They believe the Zen-like So Cal way is to let things come to you. If they do, partake. If they do not, they were not essential. Oh, okay, let me ask you this, Buddha: Did that $3,000 hand-knit, sweatshop parka come to you in a dream? Did all your silly colored rocks and sun crystals arrive on your doorstep from the Hippy Stork? No. You went out and fucking bought them like any religious nut. You chose to paw your way through bins of litter to find a matching set because your peyote circle would definitely stare and talk about you if you mixed summer *and* winter colored stones together. That shit is just not cricket in the Sect Set. I wish people would just own up to their fucking feelings sometimes. Sadly, that is just not how this board game is played.

Greed is a common facilitator for things like philanthropy as well. Celebrities compete constantly to appear the most charitable. If Angelina Jolie gives $1 million to Africa, then Madonna has to give $2 million to AIDS research. If Sting gives $3 million to cancer, then Oprah has to give $4 million to feed the homeless. Do not let these people fool you: It is all about the game at the end of the day. If it were true charity, you would not even know they were donating money. The whole point is for you to notice and take the hint: They are superstars, but they have hearts of gold. But a fool and his gold are so easily divided. I am sure there are a few who actually care about their causes, but several hundred of them are not worth the checks they pray to Allah do not bounce. Greed can make you crazy, but it will make you even crazier if people miss all your attempts to *not* look greedy.

This blinking cursor is mocking me because it is 4:37 a.m. and I cannot fall asleep. I have heavy eyes and a tired body, but my brain refuses to shut off. You see, it has not really taken me very long to write this book. It all started with one chapter done in rapid fire typing and fingernails blazing. Then I finished another, and another and another. All of a sudden I was very nearly complete. My brain was getting cocky. It was getting greedy for more words, more syntax, and more precocious punctuation. It was whispering in my ears—which I know is impossible because it resides between said ears, but accurate nonetheless—"More, more, more for me, *Me, ME*!!" That is such a catchy little bit of prose that I cannot help but keep saying it. So because my brain was greedy for more progress, here I sit in the recesses of the night, tapping sentences into my red little window to the world. Hopefully soon these sentences will infiltrate a bound bit of refined wood pulp so you too can see what happens when insomnia and creativity make your gray matter appear as a faceless voice in your head. Before you ask—no, I am not schizophrenic. I am just crazy and cannot sleep. How can I sleep with all these voices? I swear that guy sounds just like me. My greed is manifesting itself in the guises of invisible Kerouacs and Thompsons who are sifting through my thresholds like cops trying to score some DNA out of my garbage. It is a little creepy here in Tennessee this morning, folks.

That reminds me: Gordon Gekko is one of the coolest movie names ever. It is right up there with Indiana Jones or Darth Vader. Gordon Gekko is a character played by Michael Douglas in the 1987 film *Wall Street* and reprised in 2010 with *Wall Street: Money Never Sleeps*. If Ebenezer Scrooge is the grandfather of greed, Gordon Gekko is his bastard son. His philosophy is very simple: "Greed is good." Now he may have turned into a serious son of a bitch in that flick, but on its face, the theory is sound. Greed can be good if kept at bay with reason. It can push you to make a dream come true and it can help you realize that life does not have to be about suffering and fasting. But like addiction, the bad end of this dirty pool is a shipwreck all too familiar in this country. Look at Bernie Madoff. I am sure that motherless whore seed has money stashed in places we will never even think to look. There are so many strikes against this guy that I would be hard-pressed to find one that would sum everything up. But I did. It is very simple: Anyone who steals from Kevin Bacon should have his knees pushed out the wrong way. I would want to be there so I could take pictures. And also so I could take a crack at him with a crowbar.

That is an extreme case, I know, but look at all the mayhem the world market has been going through for the last four years. This came from deregulating laws that were put in place for a fucking reason. This makes the S&L scandals of the '80s look like you just lost your wallet. This is unchecked greed and they do not care. Hell, most of the goddamn CEOs are still trying to give themselves pay raises. The president wants to do something, and Congress would back him up if it were not for the fact that *they are guilty of doing the same thing.* Greed is not a poor man's sin, but it is a poor man's burden. If these fucking sycophants would stop staring at their bank statements long enough to look in the mirror once in a while, they might notice they are turning into monsters. People are losing their jobs, their investments, and their savings, which means they are losing their houses and their lives. Do these rich white fuckers realize that by raping the American dream, they have left us with a global nightmare?

Greed is not a friendly ghost sometimes. But logic would state that greed could be used as the fuel for ambition. Do not get me wrong: I have no problems with wealth. I have a problem with corruption. There are many people who have succeeded in their lives honestly (more or less), and I applaud them. This is not about my problem with capitalism. This is about my problem with egomaniacal materialism. These white-collar one per-centers are destroying healthy business instincts and replacing them with shady stock practices and illegal kickbacks, leaving us with not only a crisis of faith but also a vacuum of ethical values. And the thing that I have never figured out is why almost all of them are Republican. Then it comes to me: Republicans do not care about the country. They care about their agenda. Then again, the Democrats don't care either. If they did, they would stand up to Republican bullies and tell them to go fuck themselves. Instead, they waffle and give ground like Chamberlain trying to talk his way out of giving Hitler an Old Stranger handjob in Versailles. The only real reason that most people find themselves moving to the Right is because that party has always exuded strength and confidence. Every once in a while, Democrats stumble on a happy accident and find a candidate that can hold his or her own against the elephants, but for the most part, they have been regarded as the Pussy Party since I was a kid. So the perceived notion of strength overshadows the clear greed and lack of conscience. Two-party systems work, but they only work for the people who believe in a two-party system. There is a good bit of greed right there: The two-party system does not allow for other people to step up and do their best for the country, and when they do, like the Green Party or the Libertarians, they are painted as freaks or misfits by the major parties. So who is exempt from being greedy exactly?

I know one thing: The more people try to repress natural feelings, the more they come screaming to the surface in a darker visage. Honestly, dealing with things naturally is the only way to develop maturity and common sense. The benefits of experience far outweigh the tenor of teachings. You never know when those teachings will be laced with personal opinion. In other words, be careful who you listen to because you never know if you are hearing fact or conjecture. Common sense is not so common anymore. Here is the deal: If you do not need greed in your life and are completely satisfied with low-risk contentment, then that is fine with me. This is not a telethon for greed. But if you are a driven person who longs to make something exceptional out of your life, then why should you not do your thing? Again, greed does not always have to be a path to utter destruction. It can be a path to terrific things and stupendous achievement. It all comes down to how you live your life. Greed is a tool. Take a minute to think about that. No, it is okay—I will wait. I have to pee anyway. I will be right back. Help yourselves to chips and dip. Do not eat all of it and no double dipping. That means you, with the moustache—do not get your face pubes in my taco dip. Seriously! Keep your boner broom away from my bean dip! Everyone have enough punch? I do not know why I am serving punch at a party that only exists in my head, but fake punch is better than no punch at all, right? At least it is not a fancy-dress or a vicars–and-whores party—I am not completely weird.

Take your meds, Taylor, for fuck's sake.

*   *

On a fairly serious note, if you want to see real greed in action, take a casual stroll through any casino in Las Vegas or, for that matter, the airport or any convenience store that has electricity. If greed is a giant hunting knife, then gambling is John Rambo, using it to not only garret people's windpipes but also to sew up any pesky wounds obtained in battle with the needle and thread stored in the knife handle's trusty secret compartment. Las Vegas, at least on the strip, is a wondrous theme park with a cast of characters that any fiction writer would masturbate over. The funny thing is that people who are well off enough to gamble and lose are called whales. People who cannot afford to gamble and lose are called addicts. So who is greedy and who is an athlete? I watch the *World Series of Poker* all the time, and whenever someone goes all in on a pair of tens, I just want to smack that person in the face with my dick. Greed is never a good partner when you are trying to bluff. You sweat like a sex offender and your give away tells like a kid with AD/HD. When too much is at stake, gambling is no longer recreational. It is greed, pure and simple. Greed takes over when you are trying to break even, or at least cover your losses. Greed turns a man with a poker chip into a man with an obsession.

I have been on both sides of this. On the lighter side of gambling, I was strolling through the Rio one night and found a $25 chip lying on the floor. I had imbibed a few cocktails and was feeling lucky, so I said fuck it and muscled up to one of the blackjack tables for a few hands. I walked away with $800 even after I tipped out to the dealer and the waitress. I was ecstatic. I bought a round of drinks for some friends and managed to hold onto the rest of it long enough to buy a beat-up pawn shop acoustic guitar that I use to write the majority of my songs with to this day—a happy ending to a pretty cool story. Nobody died, nobody sold their car, and nobody felt compelled to clean out the children's college funds, so well done, right?

The darker side of gambling never even occurred in a casino. It happened about 2,000 miles from Las Vegas, and there were only three people in the game. We were playing a game called In Between, wherein a deck of cards is dealt out two at a time into two piles. For every two cards played, the betting occurs when you have to guess whether or not the next card will fall in between the previous two. Say the first card is a king and the next card is a three. If you place a bet, the next card has to be a card from the queen to the four. Sound simple? It isn't. If you catch a queen, two, and the next card is outside those two, you pay what is in the pot. If it is either a queen or a two, you pay double. It is a game that can generate a healthy money pool very quickly but, in the process, make the players pay a heavy price if they get in over their heads.

Now the great thing about gambling among friends is your odds of winning double. But the bad thing is your odds of losing stay the same. I would love to say I did not lose $30,000 in a round of private gambling, but I did. It sucks even thinking about it, but at the same time, it taught me a few valuable things about myself. For one thing, I paid up as soon as I could. I did not have $30K on me at the time but neither did anyone else involved in the game. It was the right thing to do and I am an honest person, which leads me to the most important thing: Honor your debts. It is easier to cut your losses and walk away clean than to get into the cycle of using other bets to pay for debts. I do not ever want anything like that hanging over me. The second thing I learned was that you should not gamble with money you do not have, and by that I mean do not gamble when you cannot afford it. These days I only gamble with money I have in my pocket or whatever I get from *one trip* to the ATM. It will keep you from making greedy mistakes and it will keep the fun in your gambling. By the way, I do not say gambling habit. A habit is something you do every day, a quirk that develops around your personality and your daily movements. A gambling habit is a gambling problem, and I will not subscribe to using euphemisms to cover the fact that some people have a problem with gambling. I am not encouraging people to gamble their money away; I am encouraging people to gamble responsibly and for fun.

Right now you might be asking why I paid that kind of money in the first place because it was between friends and there was no compulsion or rules to make me do so. That is very simple: honor. I know it may sound stupid to some people, but honor is to be expected as well as practiced. If I had been on the other end of that deal, I would have expected to be paid. I would have expected that debt to be honored the same way I honored my loss and paid in full. Honor goes both ways, just like greed. So if you have honor in your life, greed will never get a nasty hold on you. Greed takes a sinister turn when you dump honor by the side of the interstate like a hitchhiker that refuses repeated requests for a happy ending. But when you take the high road and respect the whims of fate, you and your wayward passenger will get to where you want to go safely and quickly.

I do not really gamble that much anymore regardless, and not because I am afraid of losing but because it is what it is: a great way to let off some steam and put a little travel on the chain I keep my own greed on at all times. My one weakness, however, is the *Star Wars* slot machines at the Palms casino. I know that is not the toughest sounding game around, but I have fun, and Texas Hold 'Em has become so damn trendy I would not want anyone to see me playing it. Not to brag, but the last time I was at the Palms, I won $3,000 over the course of three nights on those slots. I only risked $400. It was fun: My gang and I were enjoying complimentary Jack and Cokes and yelling and screaming; we were attracting spectators who wanted to see what the hubbub was about, and at the end of my stay I basically paid for half the expenses I accrued in hotel lodgings. Fun is fun; compulsion is a disaster. But greed is not to blame. Everybody I know has addictive personalities. Greed is just one more leg for those personalities to stand on. You have to figure it out for yourself in the long run.

So I guess the question becomes how stable is your grip on yourself? People have been in the market for the bigger, better, now since the bitter, better, then. Greed has its roots in the hunter and the hunger in all of us. We have it in our user manuals to want and to acquire, to earn and to take. To me, this is the fire that originally got us all going past the boundaries of our minds. What is greed but the thirst for more? That sounds like discovery. That sounds like progress. That sounds to me like a little bit of everything, right? There is a sliver of greed in every step we have taken from medieval to medical, from superstition to science. The greediest minds wanted more than myth had to offer. The masters of our universe got a taste of something significant. And even though the immensity of that knowledge made them feel a bit insignificant, it was enough to make them greedy for more. The depths of the human capacity are immeasurable, and greed makes our hearts voracious when it is bent on finding great things.

I have been greedy my whole life, but not in any way that would make me feel like a sinner or ashamed. I was greedy for intelligence, so I fed myself books and anything else I could to achieve it. I was greedy for life, so I did my very best to go out and live it. I was greedy for music, so I spent a lifetime sifting through sought-after albums and tapes, then CDs and MP3s to experience it. I was greedy for love, so I went after the most beautiful women I had ever seen, and even when we broke each other's hearts, we loved as hard as we could to feel it. There is greed in my blood. Hell, there is greed in your blood. The people who tell you otherwise are greedy for control of as many of your emotions as they can get. Maybe that does include me because I am trying to undo years of outside influence. People will think that is a very lofty statement and that I think very highly of myself. Of course I do. Why would I write a book if I were not going to attempt to change some minds? Why would I be doing this if I did not think I had a point? The naysayers are a hangman's jury of free thought and I am your lawyer. Fortunately, your lawyer has a case. No one should feel bad about their doubts especially if there are no honest reasons for feeling as such.

For now, we all go about our lives the same way we always have, with the guilt of the dead and anxiety for the unknown. Someone other than myself said that some shit, suffice it to say, just does not wash off. Maybe we are not ready to shed the stigmas of these quote-unquote sins. Maybe the decades we have spent immersed in the haughty sights of the repressed have left us all a little less likely to flip the script right away. But my one flaw has always been my one strength: I see the potential in everyone. I know the world has what it takes to do what it takes. So I will wait patiently. I will not be greedy with your time or your decisions. I know good things come in due time. And I have time. I have all the time in the world. It just means more, more, more for me, *Me, ME.*

I have time for that.

Glutton for Punishment

Did I ever tell you I used to live in a closet? True story.

I was living with my mother, my sister, my mom's best friend, her daughter, and whomever the two matriarchs happened to be dating at the time. We had rented a house outside of Waterloo, an old farmhouse on a plot of land that no one had bothered to work in years. It had a couple of out buildings, a silo, and a circle driveway I was forced to ride my ten-speed around for hours because we were not close enough to town for me to ride. Anyway, I had not had my own room since before my sister was born. So when my mom told me the new house would have a room for me, I was actually stoked to finally have my own fucking room. For the better part of four years I had been sharing a room with no less than four different kids, all of whom were younger than me. I was getting to the point at which I needed my own space. I needed a little privacy. They alluded to the fact that it was a lot smaller than I thought, but I heard nothing but my and room. So as I packed all my stuff, I was preparing what I would do: I would hang my Iron Maiden posters on all the walls and set up my radio right next to my bed so I could listen to my George Carlin albums to go to sleep. Teenagers only feel good when they are alone in their own house. I was ready to get out of the romper room and into the high school confessional.

Imagine my surprise when I landed with both feet at the top floor, flung open the heavy door and found what my new digs were. Yeah, it was a closet at the top of a staircase with no light and no electrical outlets. So even if I hung my posters I could not see them. I had to buy batteries for my radio so I could listen to my music, and they were constantly dying. Plus I had to keep it down because everyone in the house could hear my radio seeing as I was at the apex of the house. There was no heat, no windows, and no end to the dust and spiders and smells that collected in that dark, fucked up place. It was stuff like that and a host of other reasons that made me restless and reckless. I got the short end of the stick so often that I just started staying away from home.

That was when I discovered the joys of speed and cocaine. I did not want to sleep and I did not want to go home. I just wanted to run forever. I was gone all the time, and I did not really care where I was or who I was. All I wanted to do was find the next party so I could forget and feel alive. Pretty soon, I weighed one hundred pounds and my eyes had darker circles than most cult members. I was living in dirty jeans and squats between bouts of laughing at life and crying over death. I was losing friends daily. I was losing my mind slowly.

Then, when I was sixteen years old I woke up in a dumpster with no shirt and blood on my face. I was missing my shoes and I was twelve miles away from my house. I had no money, no ride, and no clue how I had gotten there. I guess that is what a cocaine overdose gets you at a party where you do not know anyone and they do not know or want you—dumped, abandoned, and bloody. The sun was blaring in my face, sending me signals that I had done something idiotic the night before. I was pale and weak. I suddenly knew how Béla Lugosi felt. So I lay in the garbage for a long time just getting my collective shit sorted before I even thought about going home. I was wrapped up in shame like a narcissistic Christmas present, praying to whomever was listening not to open me the night before. Shortly after that was when I made the decision to move back to Des Moines. For a young, fucked-up little addict, there is no better wake up call. When you try to describe addiction, I guess there is no better word than gluttony.

Now I know popular usage dictates that gluttony is mainly connected to eating and consumption. But for me, gluttony hovers somewhere between overindulgence and OCD on all levels. From hoarders to "seat smellers," the range on the gluttonous topography is a lot more widespread than I had thought when I started working on this chapter. But when you think about it, I guess it makes sense. Buffets are for gluttons. Lotteries are designed for gluttons. Stamp collectors are ubiquitous gluttons. That silly little creature in your brain that craves making every whim come true and every want become sated is gluttony. Whether it is food or drugs or material items or just comfort, you can find yourself being a glutton even if you think you are the most even-keeled person on the planet. I think we are all gluttons on the inside, but on the outside you would not catch any of us being so quote-unquote "petty."

If you were to look up the definition of "gluttony" in the dictionary, you would be surprised by how simple the answer is:

excessive eating or drinking. But if you felt like opting instead for "glutton," an interesting little subtext comes to light. The definition for "glutton" reads: 1. one who eats or drinks in excess; 2. a person with a voracious capacity for something; and 3. wolverine, in Europe. So a glutton is trying to fill a void with something, anything. Metaphorically speaking, a glutton is most likely trying to keep a beast at bay by feeding it whatever will leave it feeling satisfied. But that is the rub: A glutton is never really satisfied. No wheat or wine will fill the gargantuan pit of emptiness in the gluttonous confines of the human soul. It is in all of us. It is as universal as blinking. It is not a sin, but it is serious enough that you must handle it with caution.

Honestly, I have never been a fan of cold, totalitarian definitions anyway. I prefer thesauruses: different choices synonymous with the source word. I am definitely a little more prone to finding the 360 about anything. If you do not come at something from several angles, you will never see the overview, the 3D delicacy of everything. Whereas man—or humankind, if you want to be PC—has searched for the truth for aeons, I am more interested in finding the path first. If you do not know where you are going, how the fuck will you know where you are when you finally get there?

So gluttony for me is a lot of different things. It is compulsion and capitalism. It is sadism and masochism. It is abuse with a revolving door. It is peanut butter and chocolate on a Friday and a binge-drinking whirlwind the Saturday after that. If you are voracious and tenacious enough, you can overload your system with so much stimuli that you will crash and burn just to feel the sensation. A glutton is a pig and a pigeon. Look in the mirror, friends, a glutton looks a lot like you and me. We are a million strong and a billion counting. We are the generation that can never get enough. Why not? We are also the ones dealing with guilt trips to the past, present, and future. No one trusts the next shift, so they take their coffee and mug home after work. No one trusts a neighbor who is doing better than they are.

In all fairness, the American wet dream comes with a commercial saturated in gluttony, urging us on toward the limitless warehouses of excess. From all-you-can-eat buffets to 99-cent stores, we have made a promise to every burgeoning pack rat and strung-out sucker that anything worth having is worth having ad infinitum and with very little cost. The only problem is that you get a bill you cannot afford much later, with an interest rate that will kick you while you flounder. You can wait for fate to make its presence felt, but by that time the hunger has moved on, seeking refuge in something else. Gluttony looks like a sunburn and feels like the bends. If greed is more, then gluttony is extra. That may not make sense, but it is true and poetic: We glut until our stomachs and minds are distended. The feast is for the body and soul. If our eyes are bigger than our stomachs, then how fucking big does that make our stomachs?

I have got to be honest: There is no other sin, whether a part of this deadly list or otherwise, that is more American than gluttony. Look around you. People from the United States are some of the fattest in the universe. The world wonders why California is falling into the sea. It is because it cannot take the weight. Americans have a serious weight problem, more than any other country on Earth, which is very ironic seeing as no other nationality worries about its appearance more than Americans. We are gluttons for food, but we are devoted followers of infomercials and handy home gym equipment. You see, the thing I have realized is that sins make people stupid, not deadly. Stupid

Americans are fat, lazy, indignant bastards, but god forbid you call them fat and lazy. Americans are also, by and large, the most obsessed with amassing wealth and power. We make promises across oceans and airwaves that anything is attainable if you want it. It really explains a lot about this country.

Here is something I just realized. There are so many quirky names for gluttons, which just shows you how entrenched gluttony has become in our culture. From attention hog to ball hog, it is almost an unconscious way of accepting the fact that we are all gluttonous, wretched fuckers. We make light of things to help us forget how heavy they actually are. The thing that puts the sting in this behavior is the selfishness: You have got to be very into yourself to want to stuff yourself full of bullshit or surround yourself with a multitude of things you do not need. Once again, it is a question of getting yourself to believe the Big Lie, which is that everything you do is noble and selfless. This could not be further from the truth. We are all dirty little coffers waiting to be rammed full of our hearts' desires. So if we are all going to glut on the fruits of labor, why stigmatize the feeling? I say we all embrace the beast and move on. But nobody listens to me— my lips do not move when I think. I cannot be trusted.

Me? My gluttony is entertainment. TV, movies, comic books, books in general—I devour these like water to a parched body. But my true passion is music. I have been wading through music my whole life, even before I realized I had a knack for it myself. I have had the blessing of being exposed to music as long as I can remember. And it continues to this day: I am a voracious fanatic with a reservoir of knowledge, not only for the music itself but for the histories behind the many genres I enjoy. I want to know everything there is about the composers and the rock stars that have created my personal soundtracks. The great thing is that I learn new things every day, from the little bits of ear candy in the mixes to the inspirations behind the lyrics to the vibes behind the scenes when certain songs were recorded. I find my way through the dark with a little help from my "friends," most of whom are people I have never met. But they helped me grow up and gave me a reason to vent all my troubles into melodies and prose. I am a glutton for junk food music: Give me a cigarette and a microphone and I will sing along all night long.

By the by, I have discovered that there are many phases involved in the development of a true music connoisseur. The first phase is your early recollections of music, most likely picked up around the house as a toddler. I can remember hearing everything around my grandmother's house, from the Statler Brothers to Black Sabbath, the latter courtesy of my Uncle Alan. My mother was a fan of Motown and disco, so I had the Jackson 5 and the Village People running around in my head as well. Throw in a little bit of Beach Boys and Beatles and you can see that I grew up with major chord progressions and big harmony choruses on a Big Wheel ride to my destiny. Kids naturally grasp onto major keys because of how happy those tones feel and sound; children want to play and smile, so they want stuff like Christmas carols and Happy Birthday. The itsy-bitsy spider ran up the inner ear and into your subconscious: Do not fight it, that shit kicks ass.

The second phase of musical taste is from siblings and such, something I call the Babysitter Syntax. Especially if you have older brothers and/or sisters, you become aware of current music almost subliminally. Because I had no older siblings, my second phase came from my cousins and my babysitter, Anna. I heard everything from the Sex Pistols to Def Leppard, and I suddenly realized I was a rock fan through and through. It was visceral and dangerous and I loved it so much that I could not wait to find more. Between the two of them, I learned about Mötley Crüe and Ratt, the Damned and Adam Ant and, of all things, Journey. I was eight years old when MTV first hit the airwaves, opening the floodgates for a pop music meltdown: Michael Jackson, Joan Jett, Pat Benatar—the list is ridiculous and it was all I had for a very long time. I performed in front of my first "audience" when I was ten, singing along to Journey's "Separate Ways" for my aunts and uncles in a Spartan living room in Indianola, Iowa. What the hell did I know? I was ten!

The third phase is what I consider the most crucial: discovering *your* music. You see, until that point we are all exposed to other people's music, which is all well and good, but it stops speaking to you after a while. You need something that feels like your own. You have your own generation to stand with and that includes your own set of problems. It also means you need your own music. That is when metal swept into my life. *Master of Puppets* was and still is the greatest album ever created. It was a turning point for me. I absorbed any and all metal music I could get my fucking hands on: Slayer, Anthrax, Megadeth, Testament, even skate thrash like D.R.I. and Suicidal Tendencies. I finally had a style that was *my* style. My listening started to expand at an alarming rate.

If you are a casual listener, you usually do not make it past phase two. You saunter along with the rest of the herd, clinging to the latest mesh of pop pathology and reminiscing about times when people were not so angry or loud when they made music. If you are anything like me, you stumble onto the next few stages in your development. The fourth phase is a sort of maturation of the younger aggressive stage. I started expanding past metal after a while, going back to my punk roots and discovering this movement coming out of Seattle and Minneapolis and a handful of other places. From the Cure to Nirvana, alternative music—called "college radio" when I was listening to it—was speeding its way into the international psyche to destroy the bloated carcass that was Mainstream Rock and Pop Princess Crap. Alice In Chains and Soul Asylum steered me toward a future that was more Dylan than Dio, and I rolled around in it like a dog in a yard full of delicious bones. You could take the darkness and shape it to your will. You could basically do whatever you wanted. All bets were off.

And that brought me to my final phase: the creation and realization of my own music. I had been writing and playing my own stuff long before that, but up until that point, I had only been mimicking what I had been listening to. I was a response and call with an acoustic guitar and an attitude. It was all I knew. But when I heard "Would" by Alice In Chains, I knew there was so much more I could do and that I wanted to do. It was an expansion of the hunger in my soul that needed to sing and be. I had been looking my whole life for something to unlock the inner muse. I had finally found it. And I have never looked back. This glutton has scoured the entire musical landscape, taking twists and turns wherever the road gets crazy, from P Funk and Public Enemy to the Rolling Stones and Roxy Music. Mike Patton made me want to explore any and all vocal styles. David Lee Roth and Steven Tyler made me want to party and smile. Henry Rollins made me want to write and scream. Bob Dylan made me want to be a genius. Johnny Cash made me want to sit on a corner and smoke while singing sad songs. But James Hetfield made me want to be myself. I am a gluttonous child with the music of time in his veins. I always want more. I always want to make more. I have no boundaries and no limits—I will push the lines and blur the borders. I have not heard the ultimate song yet, but then again maybe that is because I have not written it yet. I am enough of a fan to know that you can never put limits on your abilities just as you can never put limits on what you like. I have always said your heart knows better than your head does when it comes to the music you are drawn to. If you can get out of the way of your own prejudices, you can experience a universe of music. I stopped holding myself back a long time ago, and the payoff has been rich indeed.

Gluttony has bursts of brighter sides, but the darker sides can be vicious. An abused wife who refuses to run from her torturous husband becomes a glutton for fear because her capacity for denial makes her a target. It is twisted conditioning; I am not saying it is right. I am saying it happens all too often. The other reality is she fights back and either flees or kills the man. That woman can then become a glutton for life and happiness, spending the rest of her days feeling sunlight instead of raining fists and brutality. The epilogue becomes the karma that should befall the abusive man. There are no sins bad enough for him.

I have a hard time with this whole sin thing because it is the act that carries the stigma, not the aftermath. I mean what good is a bottomless hunger if you cannot try to fill it? Ask this: Are you a glutton if you have no idea what you are hungry for? Can you suffer if you do not know why? We are force-fed this moral bullshit from the moment we take our first breaths. People judge people, and we don't need a reason, just a scapegoat. Humans have been manufacturing targets out of each other since our molecules formed. It only makes sense that we would break it down to hunger as well. What do we care? We live our own hells every day. We feel our own pain. Is it the distraction that gives a little respite? Are we truly so indignant that we sift through people's emotional trashcans to find something, anything, that will give us the superior edge? Nobody wants to feel alone in the world; they especially do not want to feel alone in their misery.

Drug addicts and alcoholics are gluttons for not only the chemicals they take but for the effects that are forthcoming. It can gloss over a different hunger entirely. Repression and delusions can only make a person long for the thrill of contentment. Getting high or drunk is meant to be a celebration, the old rituals of becoming one with "god." Visions and lightning are a heavy effect. If these things make you feel like god, why would you not want that feeling all the time? But stamina, adaptation, and tolerance can build up fairly quickly. Suddenly you are drinking more and taking more and looking for all the right "reasons." Dependency can destroy the greatest of us; so many talents have come and gone. But it is not the gluttony that ultimately kills them but the depression, and I mean that in the literal and metaphorical sense. Depression is a dark lonely place. A depression is also a hole. The parable is obvious.

I had an alcohol problem for a while. I was drinking two or three bottles of Jack Daniels a day. I just wanted to stay numb and drunk and oblivious to what I was doing so I could do something other than what I was supposed to do. I never stopped to realize that maybe I was doing it to mask something, something I did not want to face. Fortunately, it had never really affected me adversely when I was doing things like *Late Night with Conan O'Brien*, but as time went on, my darkness slowly took control. Fast forward to *The Tonight Show with Jay Leno*: I was lined up to play "Bother" with a string quintet I had never met before in front of an audience of 35 million people. Yes, I was nervous. Yes, I was unprepared. Yes, I guzzled my way through a bottle of whiskey just so I could do it. So my gluttony for alcohol, misery, and challenges all coalesced into a frothing experience that I have very little recollection of. I regret it, and I spend very little time on regrets. But this one sticks with me. I was in front of a national audience, really basically by myself, playing guitar and singing. I should have relished this moment. Instead, all I have to show for it is the cardboard *Tonight Show* nameplate from my dressing room with my name on it. I do not remember meeting Jay Leno, which I allegedly did. I have no clue if I was good or not. I have seen the footage and I still have no idea. All I remember is purchasing the Skid Row T-shirt that I wore for the performance. Everything after that is a blur. That should have been my first clue that my gluttony had gotten out of hand.

I was miserable, a broken poker player who had tried to buy his way out of too many bluffs. I was a ball of hate with whiskey in my fists. I did things I am not proud of during that time of my life, and that shame reinforces my resolve to be the very best person I can be. It took three years of being sober and another two years of being on my own to find that hunger, that black spot in the desert that the sun can never seem to get to no matter where it places itself in the sky. I have put my hungers in their proper places, and now I move a few days at a time through the remnants of a life that was almost wasted. So when I stepped onto that *Tonight Show* stage with Slipknot a year or so later, I was not petrified. I was not nervous. I was invigorated. I was there, strong and coherent, ready to show the world just how fucking good I really was. I did not give a shit if I fucked up or not—I was not going to be fucked up. So I would be myself and destroy, and that I did. I know now that my misery fueled my gluttony to speed out of control. So I do not blame the drinking. I blame myself.

But that was not the first time. I have had an addictive personality since I was young. I have noticed that the term addictive personality is a euphemism for glutton, just like custodial guardian is a euphemism for parent. I am enchanted and consumed by things very quickly. I am like a mad scientist running with a dangerous hypothesis. Maybe this is because I grew up limited by what was in my brain and little else. I always had the feeling I was not like the other kids. But I also knew I could not relate to them very easily. So I overcompensated by making myself the goofball, the class clown. A front man/showman is nothing more than the class clown on a bigger stage. So I am a glutton for attention as well. I want all the eyes on me for as long as I can hold their fixations.

Self-esteem is a key factor to gluttony. When you feel incomplete, you crave something to fill the void. Psychologists describe it as compulsive eating. That in itself can lead to the other end of gluttony, anorexia, which is a glutton's way of "fixing the problem" that gorging oneself creates. Two opposite ends of a spectrum and the result is the same: a cycle is born. Stimulus and emotional abandon will converge and yet leave you empty. So now I obsess and acquire: I buy houses, guitars, collectibles, toys and gifts for my children, and anything else that covers up the remnants of that kid who woke up in a dumpster, feeling like so much trash for the compactor. I chain smoke and binge drink and overthink and self-diagnose till my eyes boil and my chest hurts. I buy shitty T-shirts to match my shitty jeans and my shitty shoes, all so people do not notice my shitty jackets or my shitty haircut. I am a reaction in a world of practiced moves. I wish I knew who created this monster. Then again, I guess I do know who created it. I just wish the answer were not me.

So, essentially, my mind searches for distraction. There it is: I am a glutton for inspiration. I try to weed it out wherever I can, and I have become adept at it. My brain races like a freight train on rocket fuel and I forget more good ideas than I write down. I become fixated and one-minded until all I can see is the final outcome. Then all I can do is wait for the fruits to be revealed. I will get songs stuck in my head that I have not even written or recorded yet. I do not mean melodies or lyrics—I mean full-blown compositions. I can think of nothing else. I can focus on nothing else. It is the source of my greatest songs. It is also why it basically took me two weeks to write this book. When the spirit takes me, I have no control, and the spirit is all around me. The disparaging echo rattles around in my tenement and gives me a decent dose of black lung, all the while teaching me there is a sea just waiting to be established in the valleys of my heart.

When you break it down to its barest minimum, gluttony is nature's way of super-sizing the human race. People are getting larger and larger every second. I have been all over the world several times, and believe you me, it is not a specifically American problem, although pound for pound we have the biggest reputation. The global diet is fucking disgusting. We eat foods made from garbage. We eat animals that we process and inject with enough hormones to make them not so dissimilar from humans. We soak shit in fat then fry it and bread it and then fry it again. I am not saying it is not delicious; I can knock the fuck out of some chicken fried steak, especially smothered in sausage gravy and some hash browns on the side. But that is a surefire way to gastrointestinal mayhem. People are getting so fat they are having bands put around their stomach tracts to keep them from eating too much. They used to just cut out lengths of intestines, which is extreme enough, but now they put a belt around your organs, proving once again that human beings will do anything possible to keep from having to exert some fucking self-control in their lives.

Do not get me wrong—I love to eat. It is one of those plugs I use to fill my despair. I can gorge with the best of them. I once made a man who outweighed me by 150 pounds tap out at a buffet. But I know my limits, which is a perfect segue for my next example of why gluttony is about as deadly as a barbecue fart in church: professional eating contests. I know you have heard of this shit; they broadcast the events on ESPN 2. There is even an official organization called the International Confederation of Competitive Eating. It is basically sanctioned gluttony for glory and profit. Men eating seventy hot dogs in two minutes, women eating several bowls of spaghetti before the final buzzer . . . I mean people call this shit a sport. Oyereating is as much a sport as mopeds are motorcycles. Just because you get a trophy and a cash prize does not mean you deserve to be on the cover of *Sports Illustrated*. You deserve to have your fucking head examined, to be honest. It is unhealthy, it is unwise, and it is also the biggest "fuck you" to the parts of the planet living off flour and vitamin supplements. Children are starving to death all over the world. Meanwhile, John Fuckwrinkle gets a highlight on SportsCenter for eating one hundred hard-boiled eggs, breaking the record set last year by his arch rival Hank Buttertits. On this list of sins, that may be the closest it comes to actually earning its Deadly Badge. It is also one of the saddest things I have ever heard. Eating contests are just offensive, insulting, and, at the end of it all, a terrible excuse to find new ways of staying in the adult end of the competitive gene pool. Hey, Americans cannot really compete on any other level, but I will tell you what: We will kick your ass at getting fatter in seconds, huh? You are goddamn right!

The nefarious gluts of the world prey on the weak and the desperate when you throw greed in the picture as well. The real key to making these sins deadly is combining them together. Alone they are fairly blasé. But in a tag team they can become as brutal as the Hart Foundation. So a greedy glut will slip you sweet sounding words and shallow flattery while gutting your future wants for his present needs. Like I have said, moderation keeps these whims from being nothing more than human folly. But giving in and letting them take control is the real sin. There is more to life than being sated. But try explaining that to a glutton with too much time and not enough balls.

We are all pseudo-vampires dying of thirst and searching for the next great food coma. We will take anything to hold off the wolverines inside our souls. The greatest battle of our lives takes place every day on the wasted spaces of our subconscious and the innermost workings of our tragic lifestyles. We spend and fuck and eat and fuck some more and lie and cheat and take and hurt and do everything to make everyone else just identical to us. The human condition is a lot like a true crime novel. A man eats so much they have to knock holes in a building to get him to a hospital. My first response is let him fucking rot: If he could not be bothered to take care of himself, why should anyone else save him? I get very angry when I hear about idiocies and ignorance. But then I have to give myself a time out and remind myself that we are all imperfect. The idioms of the world herald a time when we as a species realize our true potential and recognize that there is only one true god: the human soul. It binds us together and gives us huge reserves of untapped power, unique strength, and infinite wisdom. I have all the optimism that this sentiment is true, but not that the idea as a widespread notion will come to pass anytime soon. If we are the "one true god," then god has a lot of fucking explaining to do.

I watch the passing of time and expectation with the eyes of someone who missed last week's episode but knows the series will not end well. We take ourselves too damn seriously. We think that everything we do is a miracle. It is only a miracle when no one gets hurt. We are common gardens with roses and weeds alike. We are exceptional with exceptions. How dare we declare that everything that everyone does is phenomenal? All we have done is dilute the juice and turn it into Kool-Aid. So it is no wonder that the volume gets turned up on things that are beneath us, such as gluttony.

Street gangs and criminals are gluttons for violence. Politicians are gluttons for power. Scholars are gluttons for knowledge. Children are gluttons for safety. Gluts are gluttons for gluttony.

What seems worse: having everything you want or wanting everything you have?

There is a famous quote that states "satisfaction is the death of desire." You would be surprised how many people get credited with that one, everyone from Bob Dylan to Steven Spielberg. Hell, some asshole even said Pete Wentz came up with it. My buddies in Hatebreed have a killer album by that name. But I believe it is one of the Dalai Lama's quotes. I happen to agree with it. The human spirit needs a healthy hunger to continue on its way toward achievement and discovery. Gluttony can stoke the fires that keep us dancing on our tiptoes, but it is hardly deadly. In fact, no one can really be satisfied. You can stop trying after you have succeeded, but you are not satisfied. After every conquest, our eyes instinctively scan the horizon for the next adventure, the next challenge, and the next reason to keep our hearts pumping red-hot excitement into our 70/30 mixture. It is one of the great gifts I accepted long ago. As long as I am still looking, I will always find myself. Sometimes that gets me in trouble.

You see, I am also a glutton for the truth. I hate fakes, shams, and liars—I always have. I cannot stand it when troglodytes ascend to heights I know damn well they do not have the talent to have earned. So I run my mouth, usually with no censor. I do not care who hears it or who takes exception. I do not give a fuck how it affects my career sometimes. I try to do my very best to call it the way I see it. Maybe that is pride or my vanity talking, but I have seen truly gifted people stepped on by ruthless hacks in the pursuit of empty credit, not actual accomplishment. When I raise my voice to protest, I am regarded as a jealous asshole.

Sometimes I feel like a leper in a health club because in every category, I categorically do not fit. That can be a scary concept late at night when all you get are silent screams of doubt and defiance. But the glutton inside is just pulling for me and mine. Something has to drive us to do our best and worst. Something has to lift our lids in the morning and keep us from shitting the bed. That something is the hunger. So before we go throwing gluttony under the deadly bus, take a look at our sweet teeth and our hobbies and our careers and our needs and realize that we have to read between the lines a little bit and come to terms with the fact that without "sins" like gluttony, our hearts' desires would be swamp grass and tasteless oxygen. Our aspirations would sink like an old Carolina brick. But with just the right amount of gluttony in our lives, we keep our hands busy, our stomachs working, and our eyes on the prize. No one can tell me that it is a sin to want something in excess, or at least no one can convince me it is a sin anyway. I know there are consequences to our actions, but when the reward is rich and the resolve is rigid and strong, this intergalactic herd of advanced apes could just be ripe for enlightenment. I have seen great things in our future, but all that can change when we stop yearning for something great, for ourselves or otherwise.

Look, I do not want anyone to be hurt or suffer. I do not want anyone to feel trapped in his or her own life. I want people to *feel* what we were all meant to feel. But I want you all to let go of that guilt you let swing around from your backs. You are carrying exponential pain, the corpses of past mistakes. You mean to tell me we are given a gift of sensation and prescience only to be treated like bastards and irritants when we try to find the boundaries for ourselves? And who said that guy who invented the Hover Chair could be named Tom Kruse? There is only one Tom Cruise by gum and he is a smiling, gnarly, rich alien psycho and I love his movies. I do not give a shit—he kicks ass. I got lost again, huh? Fuck me, I have to call someone about that. . . .

I lived in a closet, woke up in a dumpster and nearly died several times. Now I work every day doing what I was born to do. I am a glutton for my work, my passion, and my creations. I am where I am because it is never enough to have done anything—it only matters what I am doing. I love being a father and a star all at once, and I do each with the same zeal I have had for years and years. I would have nothing without my capacity for hunger. It has brought me so many blessings that I stopped counting them long ago. Now knowing that, knowing me, and knowing common sense, do me a favor and take a deep breath, slow down, and answer this question: If all that is true and amazing, who the hell can call gluttony a sin? If hunger is the root of all desire, how can that not fuel our dexterity?

I refuse to hide behind logic that dictates that normal behavior has to be vanilla and bland. I resist the doctrine that dignifies the notion of civilized decorum and that we cannot embrace our inner cravings. This kind of thinking keeps us tied to superstitions and cheapens our attempts to ascend to a better level of consciousness. Call me crazy, but is it a coincidence that almost all of these sins are the very sensations that make us feel alive? Is it me, or does it feel like ghosts from the past are still holding our puppet strings? I am sick and fucking tired of these so-called texts of faith that sell us salvation through the murder of our senses. They have no faith in the human sense of moderation. They have no faith in people. They are hypocrites. They are scared to death of their own weak wills and subscribe to believing that we are all the same. We are all "sinners." If they want to fall from grace and sell themselves short, so be it. But they can leave us alone, for fuck's sake. No one is going to shill to me a new set of standards. I am a defiant voice of sanity in the last ward on earth. Do not let them convince you that you are crazy. They are the ones twisting the spin. So they are the obvious choices to pass out the sins.

Our quiet noon in the sun may seem like a distant fantasy. Our quest for true oneness may merely be an ambling stop way off in the distance. But hope can put years back on the end of your life. The power of the mind is almost otherworldly sometimes. There are mysteries within enigmas in the future. Maybe we will never have a good answer for anything.

Me? Make no mistakes—I will be around. I will drink my double-thick shakes in triple-digit heat until they finally take my words away as well. I have no fear anymore. Why should I? It is just life, man. Life is only as frivolous as we make it. You build too many walls around it and you will find yourself locked out of your own life. If you feel like there is something better, tell the person next to you. Then tell them to tell the person next to them, and so on and so forth. Who knows? Maybe word will get back to me in the end.

Then I will rest my case.

10

For Your
Consideration ...
The New
Magnificent Seven

I remember when they changed the Coke.

I was twelve years old living in Elk Run Heights, Iowa. It was a pinky print of a town on the outskirts of Waterloo. This might be the first time anyone has ever written about it. But alas, its mention stops here. I was living with my mom and her band of alcoholics in a stout duplex across the street from a convenience store called Pronto, where I usually stole my breakfast and lunch every morning. It was there, in 1985, where I was introduced to the New Coke. I paid it little attention since we were a Pepsi household, but over the next few days I came to realize the importance of what I was witnessing. People were fucking pissed.

The new CEO of Coca-Cola kept appearing on shows like *60 Minutes* and *Current Affair*, hair slicked back and chugging gallons of the stuff. The New Coke had a new look, too—more modern than the classic design and a precursor to the labels we see today, ironically enough, on Pepsi products. The problem was that it tasted like shit. The Old Coke had a sugary-sweet slight bitterness to it; the New Coke was a combo of battery acid and Golden Griddle pancake syrup. The world was on the brink of destruction. People were fighting in the streets and appearing on *Donahue* to decry the treatment of a beloved national treasure, all of which made me smirk because at the end of the day, who really gave a one-wipe shit if they changed the flavor? Even the CEO of Pepsi came out to laud the fact that they would never change their own product, another bit of O' Henry since Pepsi had been changing and perfecting their formulas for decades.

Then, one day, a wholly different Coke showed up, sitting alongside the ever-dwindling crates of New Coke taking up space on the supermarket shelves. It was called Coca-Cola Classic and it began flying out the door with ever-growing urgency. People sighed a soda-soaked sigh of relief, knowing they had their old reliable back, even if it had been renamed and given to compensate for the mess that New Coke had stirred up. A lot of people have put forth the interesting theory that Coca-Cola used the whole scenario to help kick-start slumping sales of Old Coke, that by taking it away and providing an inferior alternative it jogged people's memories and taste buds and left them wanting their beverages back. It is actually quite ingenious, if that is what the plan had been in the first place. I am not sure I could find anyone today that could tell me what New Coke really tasted like anymore. I have my own recollection, but it is fleeting at best. I only drank Cherry Coke myself.

This business plan has not always been a failure, however. The art of replacing the old with the new has been practiced since the birth of industry. The battles between Schick and Gillette, Levi's and Lee jeans, Ford and Chevrolet are pieces of Americana. The marketplace is only as healthy as the commerce it provides, and the strength and quality of the products ensure an even playing field—fair game for a fight for dominance. Technology has advanced the speed of exceptional design. The bigger-better-now is as commonplace as the four-slice toaster and as complicated as an LED flat-screen television as thin as a magazine. We as consumers have been conditioned to insist on the latest and greatest. Reciprocation is rewarded with steady and loyal business. Capital ignorance is given a pink slip and the cold shoulder. If you do not believe, ask yourself when was the last time you tried to buy an eight-track tape.

You might be asking yourself, "Where in the hell is he going with all of this?" Well, it just so happens there is quite a bit of method among all this madness. If *Webster's Dictionary* and Monty Python have taught us anything, it is that an argument is a collected series of statements intended to establish a proposition. I am making an argument that these seven suspect deadly sins are not at all what their promo pack has promised. They are neither deadly nor are they sins; rather, they are character flaws that have been worked into every major fictional hero or villain since the dawn of literary time. But they are not sins, as I have said repeatedly and hopefully have successfully proven. Sins are just one of the many things that make us human. I truly disapprove of the idea that we are all very different. I think we have more in common than we realize.

So my proposition is very simple: We need a *new* set of seven deadly sins. We need to update our list of what bends us to scare the hell out of the rest of the planet. This new list should not only be a reflection of the adverb "deadly," but it should also be a reflection of the times we find ourselves in now. Times change and so should our notion of what sins are actually *deadly*. They should, by their own nature, be unique. In other words, they need to stand on their own terms and not bleed into one another.

This problem should be evident in the original list. There are sins here that overlap and negate themselves. For instance, I think envy can lead to sins but is not a sin in and of itself. Envy can lead to theft and murder. But just being an envious prick is not enough to burn in the Southern Hot Box. Wanting is a natural drive for us skin-covered geeks. The major duality you have to look at is the close proximity between envy and greed. Like I have said before, you cannot have envy without greed. But can you have greed without envy? See, I believe they cancel each other out. Then you have gluttony—same damn thing. You have three sins on the list that are very near to being indistinguishable. In fact, greed has tendrils that stretch in all directions like ancient ivy climbing the family homestead. It is in vanity and also in lust: The vain are greedy for the attention of others and the lustful are greedy for the sex of pretty much everyone. And any one of these can make us angry when we have no sense that we have been sated.

We are looking at this list in the entirely wrong way. We are dealing with ethereal feelings and not physicality. We are putting forth the notion that feelings are sins, and that is simply wrong. I say if you feel the need to have a list entitled the Seven Deadly Sins, then you should make it direct and deadly. And what kind of a host would I be if I did not have the answers to my own hypothetical questions? Do not answer that—I am serving my world famous Nacho Dip later. Anyway, I have assembled a new list, a morbid bunch that are not only sins but are also crimes. Some of them may overlap as well, but that never stopped the original authors from making the first list so incestuous. Prepare yourselves, dear readers. I give you the New Seven Deadly Sins:

1. Murder: besides child abuse, the most evil act you could ever commit
2. Child abuse: the crushing of the last bit of true innocence on earth
3. Rape: the vile process with which power perverts the powerful
4. Torture: another word for using might to an unfair advantage
5. Theft: the bitter byproduct of unchecked and overwrought envy
6. Lying: making truth a dirty word and destroyer of trust
7. Bad music: a vessel that elevates mediocrity for acceptance and praise

I know what you are thinking. You are saying to yourself, "You had me until you hit bad music, what the fuck, dude?" Trust me—all questions will be answered at the end, but only those submitted in writing and still only those written in blue or black ink, thank you.

Yep, these are my submissions for the new Deadly Sins, and I think they are infinitely more appropriate than the prior list. When you really look at them, the New Seven has it all: deadly consequences, sinful intentions, and terrible realities. This shit is too real not to be taken seriously. Murder in America alone has climbed steadily since the 1960s. Child abuse is staggeringly prevalent today. Rape has revealed an even darker shade of hell. Torture has become synonymous with "my country 'tis of thee."

Theft has been with us for hundreds of years, but today it is less about survival and more about profit. Lying was a pauper's folly until the rich realized they could keep better secrets from us by being deceptive. Bad music is just fucking *wrong*. These are modern times, with modern maladies. We need modern sins with modern methods to fight them. Amendments are made to the Constitution as society evolves. Why can't we make the adjustments in our Second Half so we can beat the number one defense by getting it right? Yeah, that is a football reference. Deal with it. Moving on. . . .

As I sit here, getting cigarette ash all over my computer, I realize the original list was assembled because of its delicacies and overtones. But this is not a time for nuance or insinuation. This is a time to be direct. People are fed up with innuendo and euphemisms. They want straight answers to earnest questions, and the new list should be a reflection of this. It should put it out there in bold face where the line starts and ends. The guidelines should not be inferred; lead us not into assumption. Just show us the way and we can get there on our own damn strength. So where the ancients left off, I have decided to proceed with a bit of nostalgia and a firm belief in what should be. Daylight is burning fast within the confines of our legacy. I would hate to leave the party too soon and miss out on the favors, so let's dig in and sort this out before I get arrested for jumping through the glass table, or at least before I streak the neighbors in my Red Skull mask.

Murder is the first on the block. It is the quintessential sin, really: to take a life, whether human or otherwise, out of malice or for profit or for no reason at all. It takes a lot to be more offensive or repulsive than murder. How this was not an original on the first seven I will never know. To me it is a no-brainer: If you take a life, you forfeit your own. That may be a very Right wing way to view it, but to me some shit is just fucking necessary. Am I the only one who can draw the conclusion that murder in the world has accelerated since the rapid decrease in executions? I think it is because there are no repercussions anymore. If you kill someone and you get convicted, there is a good chance you will end up with a better life than you had before. You will get fed, you will get a bed, and you will have access to an education, an exercise program, and a fairly trained physician. No one lives in fear of breaking the law. We have taken away the last consequence for taking away a life. The ultimate sin should have the ultimate penalty. I do not mean for those whose guilt is on the fence; this form of punishment has no room for ambiguity. I mean if you are guilty of murder beyond a shadow of a doubt, you deserve to die, period. You deserve to be taken out behind the shed and destroyed.

Murder is a violation of your human membership. Trust me: I distinguish between murder and circumstances like death on the battlefield or self-defense against abuse or other criminal activity. I am talking about premeditated, cold-blooded murder. There are people in this world who want to watch it all turn to ash and gray and there is no helping them—no form of rehabilitation will bring them back from the cool black of evil. That kind of numbness is a death inside the human soul, an exit of the compassion that helps us all do incredible things for each other. There are ghouls and there are saviors among us all. Keeping the ghouls around is a waste of time. If we hope to achieve greatness, we must prove there is punishment on this plane of existence. Stop leaving the judgments to a supposed divine spirit; the ignorant do not care that "god is going to send them to hell." Send them a real message: that we will not tolerate trespasses against our brothers, sisters, children, pets. Vengeance and justice are luxuries we can afford.

Child abuse is something I am even more bombastic about. Being a product of child abuse and neglect, I am very sensitive to this subject. I am almost as fiery about it as I am about murder. Anyone who mistreats a child must be made to suffer as strongly as anyone who kills is made to suffer. A child is really just a blank piece of paper at the end of the day. When you systematically break down and decimate their souls and their innocence, you kill our chances to last forever. The way some children are treated in this day and age is repugnant. We are raising a generation that will thrive on malevolence and pain. You expect us to make it to another millennium when the kids we are bringing into the world cannot even differentiate love from cruelty? I have watched the escalation of child abuse with a panic that is squeezing my heart into pulp with every offense. Who the fuck do these people think they are? They treat children like used tissue and discard them with as much ambivalence. I am horrified at the concept that with enough pain, these kids will grow up to carry on the "family tradition." The only thing that gives me pause to react is remembering one soul who came out of it with a deeper compassion for the human race: me.

There is no fate I can conjure that would be painful enough for child abusers, especially pedophiles. NAMBLA can try to sway an ignorant populace all they want, but they are still vile fucking scum. I have always believed that a society is only as strong as the ways they protect their children. I have to be honest: I have no idea how strong our nation or the world at large truly is. I see news coverage of atrocities against our young all the time. I feel the pain of the world in my chest and I am stopped dead with anxiety. Can we not all agree that we must protect our young? I do not mean by sheltering them from being kids. I mean by setting precedence and punishing those who perpetrate these acts with cold indifference to their cries for mercy. They are lower than the darkest seas and more evil than the highest form of corruption. To me, there *is* no higher form of corruption. Child abuse is a steely knife in the heart of our greatest treasures. We need to end it now.

Rape is naturally next because it is consistent with murder in that it destroys those around you and it is a symptom of child abuse as well. Rape can happen to anyone at any time. Rabid dogs in evil heat imposing their bent wills on defenseless victims, rape symbolizes a vestige left in the global psyche where men are still superior to women, where the power still lies within their grim hands. I am not saying it is a by-product of machismo; rather, I am saying it is a mental deficiency where no means yes and unchecked hatred makes a person decide to take away your choices. Rape is disturbing, and even after the physical reminders are long gone, the psychological scars linger for years. Therapy can help heal and rectify some of the damage, but the nightmares never truly go away. I know that for a fact. When someone takes away your ability to choose and to fight back, you are left bleeding and weak, shell-shocked and betrayed. When someone makes you feel truly powerless, it can shatter your heart into a million pieces. You will never look at another person the same way again. Trust may never come back, and sanity takes its time coming back as well. You are a prisoner in your own body—afraid to feel, afraid to love, and afraid to relax at all.

Rapists usually get their just desserts in prison, but, ironically, not by the justice system or the prison itself. Their punishment is served by the other prisoners. It is probably the last form of retribution left. The same can be said for pedophiles and child murderers: They receive a cruel form of punishment that makes even someone as cynical as me queasy. If that is what it takes, then so be it. People need to fear the justice that awaits them.

They need to know that there are fucking consequences for their actions. They need to be held accountable for their crimes. I have no pity for a rapist's fate. I have no pity for criminals who take innocence and grind it under their boot heels. I have no pity for people who cannot feel pity themselves. I would gladly fan the smoke from their charred carcasses with a sense that penance had been served. That was the one thing our ancestors got right: an eye for an eye, a tooth for a tooth, and a life for a fucking life. If you expect people to obey rules and laws, you have to send a clear message that there are exceptional punishments for those who choose not to. It is called prevention. It is time we upped the ante again.

Torture, our next newbie on my list, has become quite the buzzword these days. Who would have thought it would become so tied to America, a country that uses freedom as its greatest attraction? Torture is a fine choice for this list because it can be as subtle as psychological warfare and as demonstrative as waterboarding or a taste of a bullwhip. Torture is used to extract information, to justify the means and to accomplish "victory." I am not saying there are not people out there who deserve to be tortured. I think I established some wonderful candidates in my prior paragraphs. I am saying that not everyone deserves to be tortured. But innocent people are tortured every day, with little evidence and no thought to the lasting impressions. From police brutality to certain military investigators, torture has been a deadly method as far back as the Spanish Inquisition and beyond. The witches of Salem, Massachusetts, were tortured into admitting to supposed alliances with Satan and sorcery. American slaves were tortured when they did not obey or when they were hiding information on other slaves who had escaped to the North. German and Japanese Americans were tortured and herded into camps at the outset of our involvement in

World War II for fear they were spies or sympathizers. Fuck man, the more I think about it, I guess torture has been a part of American history since the inception of our country. How ironic that our founding fathers could not see that freedom would become instilled with a propensity for violent discovery.

A person who tortures lets a little bit of their soul die with every strike and every blow. This desensitizing can make us all embattled and embittered, distrustful and disruptive. Is torture the last resort of a mind that cannot let go of a preconceived notion of guilt? Are we so stubborn that we cannot accept a person's innocence? Has cynicism combined with zeal to make us suspicious enough to hurt one another? Is everyone a suspect? Is everyone's involvement just assumed so we can "prove" it through brute force and thoughtless cruelty? Sure, I have made a great case for a certain amount of universal guilt in the world, but even I am pragmatic to know that not every Muslim is a terrorist. Not every German is a Nazi. Not every banker is embezzling our money. Not every criminal is a killer. Someone who tortures is pushing us all into the meat grinder, making our entrance into deadly sin a little easier by making us all seem guilty when that is simply not the case. I would like to see how they would like it if someone hooked jumper cables up to their most tender extremities in order to extract a bit of information. I can only hope they do find out some time. The indecencies that were committed against the prisoners at the Guantánamo Bay military base are really just the tip of the iceberg. Never mind if some of those "detainees" are guilty or not—is this the face and heart of America? I shudder to wonder.

Theft almost did not make my new list. Stealing has kept me alive longer than I can remember. There really was no profit in it for me; it was just a way to eat and to impress my friends. Well, shit, I guess I profited with acceptance from my friends, but that is not the point I am going to make here. Theft has brought the world to the brink of destruction. I am talking about the high-octane, absolutely corrupted misappropriation of public and private funds that has driven us very nearly over the edge, spinning into oblivion. When the Republicans rose back to power, they began to deregulate every little piece of legislature that kept the giant greedy corporations in check. All of a sudden, monstrous debts started to accumulate throughout our cities and states. A trillion-dollar surplus was depleted at an exponential rate, leaving us with a deficit that we are still trying to recover from. Why is it that every fucking time the Republicans take power, they leave the Democrats a mess that takes years to repair? And the conservatives continue to be indignant, as though it was the Democrats' fucking faults! They let the dogs off the chain to rip our infrastructure to shreds like a chew toy in August. Then they fight every way the liberals can think of to fix the situation. It makes me so fucking angry that I cannot breathe. It is unbelievable.

The theft that has been perpetrated in this county has been felt in the farthest reaches of the earth. The fact that most of these white-collar bastards have largely gotten off unscathed and unpunished is a moral offense to everyone who believes in this country and its justice system. They should be hung above Wall Street by their scrotums while bamboo shoots are shoved into several orifices, displaying the accused and guilty in the market square as a deterrent to the rest of our people. Best keep your dishonest ways in check: The wicked will be brought to pay for their crimes, better in this world than the next. No one should get off scot-free. There is no guarantee that your "god" gives a shit and will take hostile action. Better to make it happen here so we know it gets done right.

Lying is really just part of being human. We all lie like crazy hoping we will get away with whatever it is we are trying to talk our way out of. I do not like to lie, I do not condone it with my friends, and I certainly do not tolerate it from my kids. Lies have covered up the dirty parts of the carpet in our little freedom temple here in this country. We lie to ourselves, we lie to each other, and we lie to the world. But the same defenses I have used to excuse the original sins will not do in this case. I cannot say that lying is okay. It is the tiny leak in our gas tanks, making us slow to develop and realize our true potentials. I know it is just one idiosyncrasy we all have in common. But that does not make it okay. It does not make it commonplace. It does not mean we should. Most of us cheat on our wives and husbands. That does not make it okay. Adultery is the ultimate lie because your life is false, your love is false, and you wind up with too many faces to keep up with. You cannot be a total person if you divide against yourself. I made a commitment to never lie again. I have slipped a few times since then, but for the most part, I am keeping my word.

A liar cannot be trusted, so he or she will not trust in return. That notion spreads like spores on the wind, planting and taking root across land and fruited plain. Lies create rifts in relationships, whether they be romantic, diplomatic, or otherwise. If the truth will set you free, then the lies will keep you locked in the bottom of bullshit for the rest of your life. You have to live with the results. You have to deal with the derisive nature of the people who just assume you are going to lie to them for the duration of the time they have to deal with you. You have to work harder to earn back trust than to continue it. We can all become a fragment of our own delusions if we do not maintain our words. A life is only as decent as the testimonials left behind when it is over. Your reality is never your own; it is kept by the people who talk about you when you are gone. A liar's legacy is laced with untruths. An honest man will have the good and the bad, but the truth, nonetheless, will shine on long after that person has been given back to nature.

Finally we come to the odd man out: bad music. I know there are those among you who will think I am losing possession of my faculties, but let me fill in some of these blanks for you people with blank stares. Bad music is a form of murder to the true art of music in general. Bad music forced on a child is abuse because it invariably forms that child's taste in music. Bad music has raped an industry that was held up strongly by great expression for decades but now finds itself floundering, giving in to the lowest common denominator of music just to keep its panties around its waist. Bad music tortures the eardrums and kills little bits of your senses through prolonged exposure. Bad music steals money from shallow pockets, steals airtime from more deserving bands and songwriters, and steals the spotlight from undiscovered geniuses who have all but given up on a dream because of the mediocrity of popular radio. Bad music is a lie, and yet it is foisted on the public in an attempt to turn melodies and songs into hamburgers and fries. Bad music is truly a sin because you do not have to be exceptional to make it in the music industry anymore. You just have to be good enough to stick around and be tolerated. I understand that bad music is a matter of opinion. I know that. But I am fairly confident that more people agree with me than you suspect.

Bad music is just fucking *bad*. It has infiltrated every genre. It has invaded every market. It is not delegated to any one form or type. There are glorious songs in every genre. There are many geniuses who know that money does not represent success. The lasting legacy you leave behind is what defines you. There is too much disposable music in the world today, and it is a black eye on the memories of those who dedicated their lives to making the form better. Music is not a fucking soda. It is not a fucking insurance rate. It is not a fucking T-shirt. It is the only real religion that is worth devoting your soul to. It is the last remnant of the primal scream, the funeral dirge, and the wedding march. It is the light that keeps me out of the shadows, and it is the reason my immortal soul is not in dire straits. Bad music sets forth the idea that anyone can make popular music. That is a fucking lie. It takes talent to be a true artist. Anyone who says otherwise is a fucking liar and a cheat. Plastic music melts when held up to the flames of honesty. Real music does not have to worry about the heat because it is already on fire with heart and soul. I can only hope that it goes away. I doubt it, but I can hope.

Then again, what would I have to crusade against if bad music went away? What would I ever do if douche bags like Paris Hilton and Lindsay Lohan did not get record deals based solely on their notoriety? Who would I goof on if bands like Owl City and Tokio Hotel were not smeared all over the sonic landscape? You know me—I do not like to name names. But every hero needs a villain and vice versa. Every Batman needs his rogue gallery. Mine just happens to surround me like a germ-free unit to fight off contagions. Everywhere I listen, there is some terrible hook leading to some god-awful racket. The auto-tuning is really the final nail in a coffin I would very much like to kick into the river. From Cher to T-Pain, this disgusting trend makes the human voice sound more like a keyboard caricature than any form of "singing." Now if you want to sing, all you have to do is talk into a microphone—your engineer or your producer will do the rest for you. Maybe that is the burden of sloth: Do not even give talent a thought because somebody else will do your work for you. It makes me sick.

I can make a few jokes at the expense of bad music, but there is nothing funny about the other members of my new Seven Deadly Sins. There is nothing funny about murder. There is nothing funny about child abuse. There is nothing funny about rape or torture. Stealing should be taken more seriously than it is and lying is only as funny as the context it comes in. This new list is at deadly as it gets; I am certain it has a higher body count than the previous seven. I do not care about the reasons for murder or rape or the rest of their ilk. That is a fucking cop out, a weapon in the arsenal of every shady defense attorney known to man. It is the *act* that is the sin. There are people who come equipped with the same traits from that original list and they do not kill or rape or torture or otherwise. So again, I say the *act* is the sin. Look at it from a criminal standpoint. Gluttony, greed, sloth, envy, rage, lust, and vanity are not technically against the law. You can make the argument that they can lead to crime, but now you are just fighting with semantics. In fact, the original Seven Deadly Sins are not illegal. Why? Because not everyone turns into a criminal when they feel these whims.

My new Seven Deadly Sins are (mostly) illegal. Murder, child abuse, rape, torture, and theft are crimes. Lying is a crime when impeding an investigation or if you are under oath. Even though bad music is not illegal, it has led to crime. People steal music on the Internet because they do not want to risk their hard-earned money on bad music. So these new sins are truly deadly and more sinful. These are the true rings of hell, the slippery slope leading to eternal damnation of heart and soul. They are also illegal by the very standards of modern law. It is simple common sense. These offenses truly go against the global herd. The real sins are prevalent around the world in every sense of civilized society. But law enforcement keeps them at bay. People who succumb to their deadly ways are usually held as examples. Their accountability is obvious. As technology advances, the shadows of doubt that once fell across the face of Lady Justice are lifting to prove the wrongly accused innocent and the usual suspects guilty. We are winning the fight for true judgment. But we are losing our way when it comes to the punishment.

Maybe if we elevate these crimes to the level of "Deadly Sins," we will be more prone to do what must be done. I understand that people have rights and I understand that there are circumstances beyond the control of total definition. But when someone is so heinous that they have to be locked away forever, why fucking bother? Putting someone to death who has personally revoked his or her humanity is not a crime in itself: It is reciprocity. It is the face of total consequence. It is something we need to do to get the chaos under control. I am not a champion for the New World Order. I am saying there is right and wrong, and people need to remember they are responsible for their own actions, no matter how severe the penalties in the end. For every action, there is always an equal and opposite reaction. If we do not procure a strong sense of justice now, who knows how far out of control the future will become? There should be no reward for negative behavior. There should be no gasp of consolation for the guilty. There should be clarity and calm. There should be a just response to the wrong approach.

That is my argument. That is really where I am in the world. People deserve to know that they can rest easy. They deserve to feel like those who are supposed to know the score actually do. There is reassurance in the feeling that someone has our backs. All the anxiety and distrust ebbs away until we stand together as a community, as a nation, and as a world that does not tolerate misdeeds and crime. There has to be a line. There has to be penalty when that line is crossed. I may be a man who has a strange relationship with anarchy, but I am also a soul who wants no harm to befall anyone. That being said, I think if you treat people like shit, you deserve to be treated like shit. Karma should be visited upon every person who spits in its face. You are playing with energies that always make their way back to the perpetrator.

The biggest argument against this new list will be the people who drag out the Ten Commandments and call bullshit on me. Well, I have a rebuttal for that. The Ten Commandments are not strong enough for this very reason: "commandment" and "deadly sin" have two different vibes to them. A commandment? Come on, man, nobody even uses that word anymore. Also there are ten of these things, and most of them really never get to the point. What is more, much like the original seven, many of the commandments cancel each other out. The Ten Commandments are tired fucking orders that came from a fairy tale. Jack and Moses and Jill went up the hill. Jack fell down and broke his crown and Moses came carrying two stone tablets with dictation from a burning bush. Give me a break, man. I say take the most volatile bits from the Ten Commandments and let them stand on their own by stepping into the shoes of the Seven Deadly Sins.

By leaving the confines of the language barrier infesting the commandments, you find yourself getting the gist when they are in context: These are the bits of the Ten Commandments that are deadly. These are the bits of the Ten Commandments we are not supposed to do. I know, I know—the way they are written may be fairly poetic. But the language gets in the way of what they are trying to say: *Do not do this shit.* Anyway, think about this: God purportedly gave Moses six hundred commandments but only ten have survived. So let's get the deadly parts into the Seven Deadly Sins before we lose those bits, too—you know, for posterity. The commandments are not strong enough in their conviction. Call them sins and you get people's attention. Call them deadly sins and no one misses the meaning.

As I have said, the time for subtlety is over. If people insist on a list of deadly sins as a reminder of the activities they are not supposed to be engaged in, then let that list blast forth with the sort of clarity you get from violent brass instruments and tympani drums. To me, it should come as common sense: This is the shit you are not supposed to be doing. But if people need a cheat sheet, fine. But let's not beat around the burning bush. Let's just put it out there. This new list does exactly that. Murder is a deadly sin, as is child abuse, rape, torture, stealing, lying, and shitty music. With this straightforward guide, there will be no misconception. I know I might think very highly of myself, especially that I may hold sway on how you readers might view something as cemented as the original Seven Deadly Sins, but I am just a guy who is looking at this from another angle. I am putting forth a sense of currency and a sense of who we are today. The humans I see like to know what the fuck is going on. I cannot help but back that.

We have been taught to live with what we know. We are just minions of the past, hauling baggage we have no idea we are carrying and have no clue where it came from. The duties of living are given to mistakes we never made and hamper our abilities to learn from the mistakes we are going to make. But that is the cycle: We are too busy fixing things behind us while simultaneously missing the things we are breaking in our own path. So I think we should turn around and pay attention to the road. The past is like ornery children in the backseat: You know it is a mess back there, but you have to keep your eyes on the highway. You can curse and throw threats, but nothing is going to change what is behind you—you can only control what you see. That is what I think a new deadly list can do: Give us a modern reminder with a classic tint. By upgrading the Seven Deadly Sins, we are embracing the original list as human inevitability. We are all those things—greedy, gluttonous, angry, vain, envious, lazy, and horny—and more. We are flawed and perfect. We are miracles of commonality. We just need to lift the guilt from our emotions and put it on a set of true sins. Is this perfect? Hardly. Is it credible? Of course it is.

There is going to come a time when we have to accept who we are without the assistance of religion. That will be the dawn of true faith. We leave the big decisions to invisible consultants and pray we get the answers we are looking for. You might as well flip a coin. The late great George Carlin once said he gave up praying to God and started praying to Joe Pesci because his prayers to Joe Pesci were answered with as much accuracy and frequency as those to God. He had a great point. I will not try to outdo his genius, but I will say this: Great minds had the insight to look for answers from the gods. They had the intellect and necessity to coin the Seven Deadly Sins. In this day and age, we need to look beyond the virginal approach to how we treated our instincts. If we need a list of Seven Deadly Sins, let them say exactly what they need to. If we as people are still looking for answers, we should turn our eyes away from the heavens and look to each other. I know we do not play well together—hell, some of us do not even like being in the same room with each other—but the divine lies in all of us. We are miracles. We are "god." If we shared a little more, we would not be left feeling less. We hold the keys to our own destinies. It is time we started looking for the locks.

11

The Dramatic
Conclusion

Dear Readers,

We apologize for the interruption, but we thought we should at least warn you before you went any further. You see, the author has taken poetic license a little too far in this last chapter.

What follows is Mr. Taylor's original ending. When we suggested to him it was not only implausible but also completely out of context with the subject matter, he immediately started to hurl whiskey bottles and soft toys at us in an attempt to do harm to our persons. After a lengthy discussion and a few strange requests (one being a vintage Darth Vader costume from 1978), Mr. Taylor acquiesced to our demands for an alternate ending if we first include his original. As per our agreement, here it is slightly edited for time and out of fear of prosecution. Thank you for understanding our position.

—ANONYMOUS

In a hail of glass and poisoned darts, I exploded out of the tenth-story window, spinning like Louganis in midair while clinging to the documents I had just stolen from a secret locker hidden deep within the last place anyone would think to look for information of that nature: the Capitol Records building in Hollywood, California. After a clandestine meeting with members of an ultra-conservative sect of the Moonies, I had stumbled onto the pieces of the puzzle that were about to blow this case wide open. Unfortunately, my escape was nearly thwarted by an elite mercenary team that had been hired by a clandestine adversary known only as the "Shadow Man" to keep me not only from revealing the contents of the documents to an unsuspecting world but also to keep me from evading capture any longer. Having no other choice but to hurl myself through inches of seemingly unbreakable high-rise glass, I let gravity hold me in its icy cold grip for what felt like an eternity before deploying my camouflaged Urban Parachute from underneath my Josh Groban hooded sweatshirt. As I floated down to safety, I could still hear the cursing from hundreds of feet above me, the sounds telling me that I had shot the gap and remained unscathed. I landed, bent my knees to take a little of the impact, cut my chute loose, and cast one long look up to where I had just come from. "One more for America," I thought to myself silently.

I made my way to my high-end but fairly inexpensive Toyota parked a few blocks away in a zone that had a two-hour window on Sundays and a fifteen-minute opportunity on Labor Day. So I was surprised when I noticed the ticket glaring at me from underneath my windshield wipers. Those sick bastards . . . I plucked it from my automotive sanctum sanctorum and, with a malicious grin, crumpled it into an oblong paper baseball, discarding it into a stream of water flowing toward one of the city's many sufficient drain openings. For a dangerous second, I allowed myself to watch its journey like a capsized ship on a raging rapid hurtling in the direction of the deadly falls. "One more for America . . . again," I reminded myself. I also made a mental note to explore other catchphrase possibilities.

My thoughts ran to that fateful meeting on the patio of one of my most trusted compatriots. He had brokered the rendezvous at great risk, as his wife was having friends over for Bridge and Tequila Night. So this tête-à-tête would be sequestered to the backyard and a generous portion of the concrete driveway. If my friend's wife happened to come across us while she roamed the house looking for more margaritas, we were to explain to her that "we were the caterers." As he snuck back inside to provide subterfuge, I scanned the faces of those assembled before me and, deciding against caution, cut to the quick with a hard-hitting direct question.

"What the fuck, dudes?"

"We can dispense with formalities, sir. We know who you are and we are aware of what you seek."

"Goody for you fuckers. Say what you came to say."

"We are not your enemies, sir. We fight the same cause."

"Fight? Are we going to have a problem now?"

There were ten of them and one of me—hellish odds, even for a man who was a trained master of several direct-to-video styles of martial arts. I squinted against the dying light to show them I meant business. I bore my teeth in a vicious smear of a grimace that hopefully disguised the fact that I had gas. I could not let my occasional irregularity get the best of me—not in a situation of life or death. So I continued to stare at them as if I were reading their minds, which I could if I really wanted to but I did not feel like it at that moment. That jostled something in them, for they got right to the point.

"That which you are searching for is not far; in fact, it is mere minutes away."

"Tell me."

"There is a place dark and forbidden to us, a place that takes a form so vile to our way of life we dare not describe it lest our tongues curl to black and fall from our mouths like old chewing gum."

"That is a very visual and gross way of putting it."

"Indeed."

"I need answers, damn it!" My patience was wearing thin, and as much as I would have loved to hang out and admire their matching handmade velour tracksuits, I had business that night, and that business meant . . . business.

"Wait no further, sir. Come closer, and we will give you the details you need."

That had been a few hours ago. After tracking down a building that to them resembled "a stack of plastic ass pancakes or records or something," I had broken in, retrieved the analog files, and was about to press the elevator button when I had stumbled into the Shadow Man's little surprise party. The crack squad were armed with riot guns and scatter shot. I had just enough time to see them thumbing back the safeties when I made a beeline for the nearest window. Now I was on the street and ready to run.

I swung behind the Toyota Celica's wheel and fired it up fast. The Toyota, or Myrtle as I had affectionately christened her last week when I rented it, jumped at the chance for action. I threw her into gear and sped to the only place I knew that was safe, the last place on earth that a gang of merciless killers would think to look for a rogue fugitive with sensitive materials they were trying to retrieve: the Starbucks on Franklin. But I could not find it on my GPS Points of Interest setting so I was obliged to head for the Rainbow Bar and Grill. Just enough time to tuck myself upstairs and out of sight in the upper bar, but that posed a problem, one of utmost importance—I was getting extremely hungry. If I decided to eat there I would have to go downstairs to the restaurant, as there were no tables suitable for dining in the upper club. And in all my years of frequenting the joint, I would not let a little thing like the threat of assassination stand between me and their world-famous Chicken Caesar salad.

But there would be time to figure out what I was going to order later. I slid my cell phone from my jacket pocket and dialed Gorby's number. Gorby was my tech specialist and I knew I would need his help now more than ever before. Skilled in every form of digital defense known to man, he would help me maneuver through the next few obstacles with a few keystrokes and some savvy pieces of advice. "Come on, man, do me a solid," I muttered under my breath. After a few rings, he answered. "Hello?"

"Gorby, it's me!"

"What the fuck, dude?"

"No time for that now. Listen, I have the documents."

Silence. "Uhh . . . what documents?"

"The secret documents I got from the meeting with the Moonies!"

More silence. "What is a Moonie?"

"I have everything I need to bust this case wide open!"

"Dude, are you high or something?"

"Gorby, I do not have time to explain. I need your technical wizardry on this. Do me a favor and go to the computer."

There was deafening quiet as he performed the task. Seconds felt like prison sentences. "Damn your eyes, man! Hurry!!"

"Okay, what do you need?"

"Look up the restaurant menu at the Rainbow, would you please?"

*   *

Dear Readers,

Once again we apologize for yet another interruption, but we could not take anymore.

That was the extent of the original ending we felt obliged to allow out for public consumption. As you can tell, though slightly entertaining, it is almost too strange even for us. You should see the rest of it—at one point he has himself in a dirt pit fighting an ostrich and an elephant that have, of course, been equipped with weapons. Fear not, PETA—they were unharmed in the end and were obviously being controlled by the Shadow Man, who turns out to be the ghost of Don Knotts for a reason that is never explained.

Artists, man. . . .

Anyway, here is the alternate revised ending he promised us, and even though it has no explosions or deadly animals, we are sure you will enjoy it just as much. Once again, thank you for putting up with this last chapter.

—STILL ANONYMOUS

So that is my book! I know you are complaining that there were not enough photographs of Betty White, but I personally do not know Ms. White so pictures of her in my book would not make sense, nor do I know who represents her at this time, although

I would love to work with her! Her role in *Lake Placid* was fucking hilarious! Shit, where was I. . . .

Dear Readers,

   Apparently Mr. Taylor was not listening when we cautioned him against this the first time. We have contacted him and he has again promised to reign himself in and finish the book in a more appropriate manner. We apologize to Betty White for her reference in what could have been a promising ending . . . although we do have to agree that Ms. White did indeed kick a lot of ass in—. Her one-liners are priceless! Shit, where were we. . . .

   Oh yes—here is the real ending and we hope we do not have to interrupt again.

                                      —WHO ARE WE KIDDING?

So that is my book! I truly hope you enjoyed it. I know it was heavy in some spots, but life happens, you know? The episodes I described all happened, for whatever reason. I have no regrets for living through them so you should have no regrets for reading about them. I do not know if you noticed, but it apparently did nothing to dampen my enthusiasm or my optimism. I am a silly bent genius with crazy fingers and antsy legs who craves attention and loves an adoring audience. And if there is anyone out there who is incredulous at the fact that this skinny Midwestern fuck up is successful, you are not alone: No one is more surprised and bemused about it than I am. There are days I still cannot believe I get away with some of this shit. There are also days when I truly believe my karma has caught up with me and I can feel the kick in my nut sack. Then again, maybe that is what qualifies me to write this book. You cannot write a book about birds if you have not studied them in HD for a prolonged period of time. So, consequently, you should not be able to write an entire rambling homage to the Seven Deadly Sins without wearing a few of them on your shirt like Cub Scout badges, right?

Besides, my "sins" are well under control, at least as far as the old seven are concerned. No gluttony, no greed, no rage (well, not much), no vanity, no sloth, no envy, and no lust—well, maybe just a hint of lust. So I am doing okay right now. But that is not to say I will not be awash in these and other human consistencies on another day in the near future. As I have alluded to elsewhere, our idiosyncrasies are what make strangers seem like family. I know one book is not going to make a dent in the theocracy that is planet earth. Hell, I am fairly certain the first thing NASA will do if we colonize the moon is build a fucking church there. I can see the taglines now: "Our congregation is closer to heaven than the rest!" Dear sweet-gravy Jesus, not for nothing, but most times you religious folk are really fucking annoying. I am dangerously close to plunging back into the old seven, and I would hate to lie to you at this point, so I will just keep my cool at least until the last page. But once the book is finished, I make no promises.

I am also nowhere near the New Seven, except for maybe the bad music, but now you are just getting into semantics and that is thankfully a matter of opinion. I am not a hit with certain people, but to each his own. I like it, so fuck it. In all seriousness, I have never killed anyone. I have never raped anyone. I have never nor will ever harm a child. I have not stolen anything in a long time. I have not lied to anyone I really care about since 2006, and I have never tortured anyone who did not deserve it. I am a creative force with a hungry intellectual chasm so I am prone to distraction and immersion in ideas and unsung music. I can get stuck in my own head sometimes, but I have become very adept at pulling myself back to Life as We Know It when it comes to my children, my wife, and the rest of my family at large. Call me kooky, but it seems like I am doing pretty good for a person who once stuck his dick in an orange for $26. Don't judge me—it was a Halloween meet-and-greet backstage. Besides, they paid me in change, those cheap pricks.

As for Dante's Infernal list, it has been dissected, dismantled, and debunked to the point where there is not much dirt left to kick in its face. I am proud to say my first book may become my favorite; if I am lucky to write more, they may suffer in comparison. Even if my grandmother is the only person who buys a copy, I stand behind every word. Knowing my Gram, she will buy a hundred copies. She did the same thing when I was selling candy bars for my bowling team years ago. Plus she took all the order forms to work with her and bullied all her co-workers into buying a shit ton as well. You have to love a devoted grandmother, people. She is the best person in the world to me. She will object to the raciness and obscenity of this book, but that will not stop her from loving me, being proud, and cleaning out the nearest Barnes & Noble. And as a good heretical grandson, I will bake her a cake on her birthday.

Look at me: assuming my first book will be in Barnes & Noble. Maybe I am a little more vain than I thought. But hey, fuck it. If you are going to have expectations, you might as well have gigantic ones. There is the old adage "expect the worst and hope for the best." That is a good way to look at life. So I hope my book makes it onto a few shelves. But I expect it will end up burnt in some Lutheran parking lot. It would not be the first time I had a burning sensation in a church driveway. Yep, I said it. I will spell it: C-L-A-P. I will take "Unexpected Sexual By-products" for 400, Alex. I just pray to Allah it is not the fucking Daily Double.

＊   ＊

Anyway, in conclusion, with all due respect to the plaintiffs, defendants, judges, juries, evidence, and impassioned debates established in the literature therein . . . what the bloody fuck do I know? I think I have made it painfully obvious that when I am not talking out of my ass, I am pulling miracles out of it. So why the hell should any of you even give my misguided musings a second fucking once-over? Well for starters, I have firsthand experience. I have no degrees, no diplomas, no doctorates, or any other slip of paper that is mainly used to make other people feel superior to others. I guess I could have printed at least one sketchy credential out and forged some signatures, but that would not be very honest. Plus they would clash with my Miss Piggy collectors' cups that I have given valuable knick-knack space to in my living room. Seriously though, I have seen a lot and I have learned even more. I can make educated guesses with the best of them. So I am nothing more than a professional observer, an armchair journalist, and a cynical fuck. But that does not mean I am wrong. In fact, I know I am not.

I know me. I know how worked up and completely hyper-caffeinated I can get, and I know that may cause poop disguised as theorems to fly from my lips like brown little epiphanies that smell as sweet as they sound. And honestly, what the fuck do I care? On too much coffee and too many cigarettes, I can expound with my fellow Irish poets and laureates till they sound last call and send us staggering drunkenly into the streets of Limerick, still going on and on about the romance but still clinging to the common sense. I do not let little things like perception or social status keep me from giving it large and telling it like it is. I would rather believe I can learn the truth than cling stubbornly to an antiquated opinion. There are enough of those acerbic hypocrites around without me helping to swell their ranks. You do not believe me? I can prove it. You know those crotchety racist pricks at the shitty bar your mom goes to? I rest my case.

A good guess is just as good as a straight answer, and a straight answer would be "maybe he is not that far off with some of this shit." It only takes common sense to sort through the recycling bin on the curb of life. And I may not have much, but I would like to think I earned my common sense badge through trial and error. If I were a real author, or at least if I were not constantly dressing as a pirate while this book was being written, I might actually concede that some of these traits are in fact not what I would call "positive behavior." Believe me, I have the scars to prove it. If that is not selling you at all, let's just put it this way: I have not jumped into any more ceiling fans and I will not be lying down in any bathtubs in Pittsburgh any time soon. So I have at least figured out that these big dogs will hunt the life right out of you if you do not keep them in check. Fair enough? Fair assumption? Fair game? Fair play? No? Aw, go fuck yourself.

I guess I will end this tawdry little tome the same way we came in, by sharing a quaint moment I experienced a while back. It was May 15, 2008. I was in L.A. doing some songwriting with a band called Halestorm. That night I was planning to do a show with an all-star cover band called Camp Freddy. It turned out to be the night I met my future wife and the night I remembered what it was like to be on a stage with no other feeling but sheer enjoyment. It was truly incredible: We jammed, we danced, and we tore the roof off the Roxy. After the club had cleared out and the energy had died down and someone finally took the J.D. away from me, a bunch of us ended up at the diner in the Standard Hotel. My future wife actually dropped me off there. As she drove away, I vowed that that would not be the last time I saw her and, after checking my phone to make sure I had truly stored her number in it, I stumbled past the seemingly unnecessary velvet ropes in the valet parking area and into the restaurant.

It was dimly lit and eerily quiet for Hollywood at 2 a.m., but that did not stop me from having an Algonquin Table moment once I was inside. Jerry Cantrell and Mike Inez from Alice In Chains were there as well as Lars Ulrich from Metallica. We were sitting at a table, talking shop and shit and anything else we could think of when the half dozen cocktails I had partaken finally caught up with me and I decided it was time to head back to my hotel for some sleep. I stepped outside past the clubbers and scene freaks parading through the lobby. But I suddenly opted against a cab. Tonight was not a night for sitting in the backseat. Tonight was a night for getting a feel for the landscape spinning around me. So I slipped my jacket on to kill the chill and, tapping out a Marlboro into my eager hands, proceeded down the street into the city.

This was Hollywood—unfiltered, unadulterated, and unflinching. I had spent a lot of time there over the last ten years. I recorded my first major album there. I had my first taste of fame and all the excessive trimmings that come with it there. I had dirty sex and whiskey-drenched adventures and violent outbursts all over this fetish wonderland. I had taken every chance and risk, transforming into a vagabond rock star. But I was aimless and crazy. I was blending in more and more with the very elements of Hollywood that I despised. I suddenly had so much in common with people I had never felt akin to in my life. So my long road back to reality came with high prices and low self-esteem. I had to dismantle an ego that was growing out of control and start from scratch. I had been famous pretty much since I was seventeen, at least on a local level. I was used to infamy. I was not used to spiraling into madness for no other reason than to see what the abyss had in store for me. I wanted more than *Behind the Music*. I wanted the Rock and Roll Hall of Fame.

As I kept walking, all of these hurdles ran through my mind. I was the Rosetta Stone, a keyhole between two worlds that needed to coexist if I was going to survive. I made peace with my demons and held onto the grudge against my angels. I remembered my goals. I remembered my dreams. I remembered myself. It was like coming out of a coma. Suddenly the orgies and the booze and the flattery and the money and the bullshit did not matter. What mattered the most was the fact that I was back on the road toward my own immortality.

I found myself sitting on an old stone bench on Sunset Boulevard, smoking a cigarette and smiling, watching the traffic roll by me. For some reason it had just come to me to sit right there, where so many had before, and reflect on that night's events. But my memories were not stuck on that particular evening alone. As I inhaled the smoke, my vision was sweeping back and looking at the culmination of three and a half decades of my life so far. I had lived in poverty and survived long enough to sit and have breakfast at 3 a.m. with people I grew up idolizing. I had suffered the wrath of karmic justice but had seen a rebirth come in the guise of great opportunities and a little positive reinforcement. I had committed every sin imaginable on a list as old as time, and somehow I was perched on a concrete slab reveling in the good fortune my efforts had sown. I was unscathed and relatively none the worse for wear, and I was in control of my own destiny, which is strange because I had always had doubt about destiny; I had seen and felt too many examples to the contrary. But there I was, a silent king on a languid street taking stock of my blessings and letting go of my curses like the smoke I was blowing into the dark. I was a ghost from the middle of nowhere. Now I was a soul on top of the world.

I let my guilt go like a handful of dust on a strong breeze. I have come to accept myself for what I am: human. I am not perfect. I am not immune to fate, but I am not automatically doomed for being alive. I feel temptations every second of every day and I am not controlled by them. I do what I want anyway, so who is to say I want anything else? When I want, I let these peculiarities run across me like dogs to their masters. When I do not, I keep them at bay with my will and my testimony. I do not cut myself off from what makes me feel; I just refuse to feel anything that cuts me off from what matters most. It is called will power. With a little practice, you can accomplish great things.

So let me clarify in a few words what I have strived to convey with this entire book: The Seven Deadly Sins are *bullshit*. They are ancient guidelines from a simpler time that have outlived their menace. In the wrong hands, they are just more weapons used to lord over decent, simple people who are trying to live life with the least amount of drama as possible. Humans will always be prone to taking advantage of any means to feel better about their downfalls. Deflection is the biggest trait of denial, so believing you are better than everyone else is the most deflective form of ignorance. Selfish malice is as genetic as the brow line we get from our parents, but what this species does not need is more ammunition to fire on our fellow earthlings.

The Seven Deadly Sins are character flaws for a reality show that has been on TV since time began. When we do anything more than silently accept them, we put unneeded emphasis on things that we all deal with but have no need to debate anymore. We are human, people! Get used to it! Instead, we waste years, even decades' worth of time on other people's garbage, using a moral meter stick that was last relevant when people wore robes and sandals to be chic.

We all travel through the hallways of life looking for the right doors, but we never check the handles in front of us; we are always convinced the exit is around the corner. It has made me believe that too many of us spend too much time either worried about the past or fretting over the future. No one truly embraces the now. No one stretches their legs out and snuggles down in the moment, that moving dot between A and B that lets you know *you are here*. Our focus has become a system of what has happened and what might happen, and this inevitably leaves you missing what is actually happening. The same goes for this tired grocery list of outdated dogmatic sins: The sweat from the stains has not even dried on our actions and we are so busy rushing to classify them that we forget to let some shit slide every now and then. Just because we might act like assholes sometimes does not mean we are defined as assholes forever. We can accept what has been done and accept what will be so we can pay a little more attention to what we are doing. There are people in this world who are going to demonize everything we do for the rest of time; let them be miserable if they want to. We will have our parties and they are not invited. If there is one thing that will never ever change, it is simply that you cannot and will not please everyone. That is a fact—trying to do so is an exercise in limp futility, and the only person who gets screwed in the end is you. Get used to giving yourself a little slack, man. Besides, who can you possibly be pleasing if you are not happy in the end? Does anything else matter past that?

Things can get tough out there. I am in no way saying life is easy and we should breeze through it like a fart through a silk filter; we are going to take our lumps and deal with our own unique adversity. What I am saying is that in all the chaos, remember to breathe, remember to smile, and remember that the only time to panic is when there is truly no tomorrow. Fortunately for the majority of us, tomorrow will always meet us in the morning with a cup of coffee and a fresh deck of cigarettes, ready to crack its cocoon and mature into today. So ease the grip on your moralities and be yourself. Fantastic is really just the flaws. Nobody is perfect—not you, not me, not Jesus, Buddha, Jehovah, nor God. But the great thing is that you do not have to be perfect to be alive, and that is what makes life absolutely perfect.

Do yourself a favor. Every night, before you go to bed, run down a mental list of everything you did that day. Check these so-called sins against it. Do not be as dramatic and drastic as most zealots or purists would be—just a quick skim across your moral waters. If at the end you do not feel like you have to turn yourself into the police or practice self-deprecation or, what's worse, flog yourself with some kind of cat o' nine tails under some weird religious doctrine, then fluff that hypoallergenic pillow, rest your head and sleep like a saint. If you left everything on the stage and all the bodies in dark alleys, then what is the problem, right? It is hard enough when people preach the way they believe you are supposed to live at you. Do not beat yourself up for no good reason. People are like pants cuffs: They can come clean with a little effort. But the longer you hold onto shit, the tighter it holds onto you.

We are all connected by unseen threads and unbidden desires, distant relatives in a massive family in which no one looks alike but we all seem the same. If music is the universal language, then sins are a universal birthright. We earn our sins through mistakes and rapture. We earn our humanity through our ability to mend. This is why when a person commits true atrocities against the species, they lose their right to claim colors. But the brutality of the extreme is as the lull of the unspectacular: rare and ultimately too coarse for common consumption. The majority of us just want to get home in time to enjoy a moment to ourselves. Do not waste one second of that time on dilemmas that hold as much water as a shot glass. Let yourself be alive, for better or for worse. Give your mind and your soul a little credit—they can take it. We are as resilient as we are reticent. There is one statement I want you to keep after you are finished with this book. It is more of a mantra, really. Nonetheless, let it crawl across your mind any time you feel you have been backed into a corner spiritually. It is very simple: Live your life, no matter what that life is.

Take that with you.

Live your life.

No matter what that life is.

12
chapter

After the Credits

I'd like to start this chapter with a fucked-up story to put everything in context of how ridiculous the people of this planet can be sometimes.

It was 2008 and I was enjoying a few days' break from the Mayhem Festival, traveling to Los Angeles with my soon-to-be wife and meeting up with my soon-to-be sister-in-law so we could go see Camp Freddy at the Viper Room for a benefit to raise money for a cancer charity in the name of a close friend to that band. My wife was still doing work for Freddy every once in a while, so it was also an evening of business for our little band of fun seekers. After she had packed up her work rig, we all climbed in our Mini Family Cruiser and headed for the corner of Sunset and La Cienega Boulevard.

The place was packed; it was assholes to elbows with . . . well, quite frankly, assholes. But spotting a few friends out front, we gained entrance to the tiny club. Seeing Billy Morrison, co-founder

241

and guitarist for Camp Freddy, he immediately coerced me into jumping up to jam on the last song of the night. I told him my throat was a little shot but I would readily play guitar. With that in place, we entered and grabbed some real estate in the corner booth by the stage with the rest of the guests for the night. I was still drinking at the time, so my sister-in-law and I began helping ourselves to Jack and Cokes fairly rigorously. Unfortunately, I found out the hard way why she was also nicknamed "The Spiller," because within an hour or so, I was wearing at least three beverages and witnessed another get dumped unceremoniously into a lesbian's misplaced purse. However, this is not why I'm telling you about the night in question here.

The real shenanigans were about to happen onstage.

As the ritual goes at Camp Freddy shows, their flamboyant lead singer Donovan Leitch would announce the guests before they took the mic from him. This night, however, Dono jumped into the crowd and stayed gone until well after the song had ended. When he returned, he grabbed the microphone and said, "Hey! Look who I found at the bar!" After that, the special guest mounted the stage and we all lost our minds.

Legally, I can't tell you who she is. I put forth the argument that since there were other people there to attest to the honest portrayal of the following events, I should be able to reveal this person's real name. But I was outvoted. So we will christen her Sherry. Sherry is very-well known to aficionados of rock and roll—a living legend as it were. I was equally stoked when she took the stage, screaming her real name and jumping up and down like a fanboy at the premiere of a new Star Wars movie. My jubilance was short-lived, however, as the following events unfolded. But the writer in me was fucking ecstatic.

Sherry jumped onstage and it quickly became very obvious that indeed she had been at the bar—for a *very* long time. Her inebriation was so plain that I exchanged a sidelong look with my sister-in-law and settled in to watch with undisguised glee. Sherry immediately started berating the audience, telling the lesbians in the crowd "how much you'd all like to fuck me, wouldn't ya?!" She then launched into the first of many a cappella versions of "Can't Help Falling In Love" by Elvis.

The boys in Camp Freddy let this happen for a few minutes, until finally Dave Navarro claimed a microphone and said, "Hey Sherry, remember this song?" With that he launched into one of her biggest hits, which she cheerfully started singing to the joy of the band and the crowd. I will give her credit, she may have been shitfaced, but she nailed that song, giving it everything she had as if nothing had happened. The wonderful performance ended to the roar of approving applause that lasted several seconds. I believe this is where everything backfired, because it became apparent that Sherry had no wish to leave the stage. Being professionals, the boys in Freddy let her stay for their version of David Bowie's "Suffragette City," one of my favorites. This quickly turned into a mistake, because it appeared Sherry didn't know the song. The only words she knew were "Hey Man" and "Suffragette City." So Dono jumped in and kept it together, with Sherry providing sparing and broken backups. When that song ended, her tenure was supposed to be over. But Sherry wasn't going anywhere. Once again she launched into her musicless version of "Can't Help Falling In Love."

Her guitarist was in the audience and jumped on the stage, grabbing a guitar and gamely trying to get the band to follow him on the Elvis song. But they didn't know it, nor did they want to play it. After a few minutes, they slowly but purposefully tried to get Sherry off the stage. She had other plans, defiantly turning on the crowd again lashing out with drunken malice on anyone "who wanted to eat my pussy!"

In the ensuing confusion, her attention came to rest on Mr. Navarro, who was watching uncomfortably. "God, you're so fuckin' sexy . . . " she slurred. "I'd love to suck your dick." With that, she dropped to her knees and, much to the chagrin of Dave and the band, began to yank on the zipper of Navarro's pants. At first, Dave was incredulous, too stunned to do anything. But snapping back to himself and with a wry wit that would only do for this surprising moment, Dave leaned toward the mic and said, "Fuck it, get *in* there, Sherry!!"

The whole place erupted. I couldn't believe my fucking eyes. Here was a woman, a rock star I'd been listening to since I was a kid, trying desperately to suck the dick of a man I'd *also* been listening to for a very long time, live for a studio audience. All we would have needed was a laugh track and the cast of *Friends*. Sherry got Dave's fly down, but not before Dave was able to fish the wireless microphone through the opening of the zipper in a very suggestive manner. Seeing the mic there, Sherry stuck half of it in her mouth and began to croon, "Wise . . . Man . . . Say . . ." They were finally able to get Sherry off the stage and out the door, but the one-liner of the night became, "Hey, be careful what you say or Sherry might try to suck your dick!"

There's a reason I'm recounting this story for you. It's a very surreal example of how your expectations for what will happen—with anything in life—can be so far off base that it makes you question if you ever really get anything right in circumspect at all. I could not have predicted for you that I would have witnessed a bona fide rock legend trying to perform oral sex on another rock star in front of God and everyone if you'd held a gun to my head and compelled me to act as a modern-day Nostrodamus. And the same can be said of the reaction to *Seven Deadly Sins*.

The book was released . . . and apparently all Hell broke loose.

My grandmother read it and cried. My mom read it and denied it. My wife read it and almost threw up. My friends read it and nearly pissed themselves. My peers read it and couldn't believe I didn't use a ghostwriter. The critics read it and said it wasn't "juicy enough," whatever the fuck that means. I told them if you want literary Chlamydia, read Tim Tebow, for fuck's sake. I don't know how people misunderstood the topic when it was *right in the damn title*. I told them it was *not* a tell-all; it was an essay-like think piece. But people don't really want to know the truth. They just want to hear what other people think, then cut and paste that opinion all over Hell and back.

But then that's when shit *really* got weird, as they say.

As I proceeded on my book tour, funny things began to happen. A woman in Birmingham, England, accused me of being too Jewish—a funny observation seeing as the outfit I was wearing on the cover was not only Catholic, but also so very clearly a costume. After standing in line at a book signing for like an hour, she launched into what I can only describe as a blatantly bigoted and obviously oblivious diatribe, condemning me for being a part of a "worldwide problem controlled in secret by you hook-nosed devils." I didn't even bother to tell her I was not a Jew. I just instructed security to "get the crazy racist bitch out of my face."

It didn't stop there. Another woman in London complained to the staff at Waterstone's that the cover was offensive and it should be pulled from the shelves. "If you want to sell this type of book, keep it behind the counter where my children can't see it!" That was her solution to a problem she couldn't even detail, made more baseless by the fact that both her children were still in strollers and couldn't read.

A man in Toronto was convinced I had written a tome about conspiracy theory and one-world government, following me around relentlessly, desperately trying to get me to admit that I "knew what was going on! Come on, man, you're famous! You've seen the proof, right?" And then I was told my book had hit #50 on the Christian reading list, which meant three possible scenarios: 1. the Christos were buying them in bulk to burn in effigy; 2. I was finally fulfilling a dream of warping the shit out of their conservative closed minds (I savor the thought of one Christian teen asking a pastor, "Sir, what's a Hawaiian Monkey Fuck?"); or 3. I was making a dent in the armor that is mob mentality and righteous indignation.

Shit, on second thought . . . it could have been all three at the same time.

But despite the incredible success the book has achieved and the overwhelming response I received on the road during my spoken word/acoustic tour—An Evening With Corey Taylor— the one thing I am disappointed about is the fact that during the extensive Q & A's I held, no one asked any questions about sin. The book had been meant to start a conversation, to encourage people to question these vice-like precipices and get us scooting on our butts towards the next level. People only really asked me about Slipknot, Stone Sour, Velvet Revolver, Daniel Tosh, Rick Rubin, Scott Weiland, and why I would ever want to hit Cher in the face with a shovel. Not bad topics, truly—I'm fairly certain there isn't a celebrity within a million miles I didn't take a shot at, which is why I'm thinking of changing my name legally to

"Google Alert"—but I had hoped for more philosophical or controversial questions about faith and dogma. Don't get me wrong, I really loved all the questions and I enjoyed answering them. I especially liked telling people about the Lindsay Lohan *Playboy* spread before it hit newsstands ("I haven't seen that much airbrushing since I was at the Iowa State Fair."). I guess I was just waiting for questions that would never come.

Then again, maybe that's a good sign! Maybe I did such a good job of making my point in the book that there was no need for overdoing it. Call me an over-achiever, I guess. The point was to scintillate, not titillate. I did, however, get some great feedback on Twitter. One person told me I could do better than this, claiming "the reason these are sins comes down to pleasure— the sin comes when you take joy in the sensation." This person obviously missed the point entirely, because that *was* my point: the Seven Deadly Sins are not sins, but they can lead to sin. Just don't blame the emotion. So are you going to sit there and tell me you should get *no* pleasure from lust? From sloth and greed? It's just another great example of the layers these "sins" are wrapped in, ensuring people feel bad for feeling, period. If I can't find a little joy in everything I do, then what's the fucking point? Now, if you apply the Joy Theory to my New Seven Deadly Sins, then I concur completely. It just doesn't hold water in the original lineup.

I got the publishing company to let me do an audio version, and, let me tell you something, I learned about a whole new wing of Hell. There is nothing more boring or excruciating than sitting in a chair, with a microphone, reading your *own* book. It also hipped me to the fact that I write sentences that are great to read . . . silently. When these same sentences are read aloud, they become a searing pain in my Man Pussy. I found myself stopping, backing up, and rereading damn near every sentence, several times. The only fun I had was messing around with the first ten minutes of the last chapter, writing adventure music and using silly voices—the whole reason it was written as such in the first place. Ironically, that was a whole section the publishing company wanted to shitcan right out of the gate. Thankfully, I held my ground and when they heard the audio version, it finally made sense to them.

I got to do some pretty cool shit in the time after the book was released. I spoke at Oxford University. I recorded songs with everyone from DeadMau5 to Dave Grohl. I roasted Zakk Wylde and helped start a film company with my brother Clown. I was able to raise money for various charities, from the Teenage Cancer Trust to A Drop in the Bucket, which helps provide water to the people of Africa. I took the stage with Slipknot for the first time since my brother Paul's death and we found the courage and love to carry on. I know I preach about no regrets, but my one regret is that Pauly wasn't alive to see my dream of having my first book published realized; he would have loved it.

As I traveled the world speaking to people and doing interviews, I realized my New Seven should have been a little longer. Instead of the New Seven, I should have made the Heavy Ten. Sure, my new list was perfect—concise, to the point and loaded with common sense—but there was room for a few extra dinner guests. One of my friends suggested I should include willful ignorance, so there: willful ignorance. I whole-heartedly agree. It is one of the worst things we suffer from in this country: when we have the information and we clearly and steadfastly turn our back, that's willful ignorance. When an individual will agree with what is right and real, but then change his or her mind when confronted with the same problem in a group setting, that's willful ignorance. When you care more about the person than what that person is actually saying, that's willful ignorance. I have no pity for a generation that will blatantly discard the truth for a false prophet with a better hairdo; if the truth is there, it must be reinforced and spread to the people.

Hypocrisy would have been in the Heavy Ten. I actually mentioned in passing that it was "to me, the worst sin of all" in the original texts. I truly loathe hypocrisy because it is the worst thing to happen to truth outside of an actual lie. The hypocrites of the world just *love* to rub shit into your face and moustache. Newt Gingrich is a prime example of the All-American Hypocrite: the brave, know-it-all defender of conservative ways and family values . . . oh, who by the way made millions upon millions from Big Business kickbacks and has been married three times and divorced twice. He even discussed divorce with his wife whilst she was recovering from cancer surgery in hospital.

* *

I guess that explains a lot really. Why should high levels of hypocrisy surprise us in politics and candidates when we are nothing more than horse shit hand grenades ourselves? That is a great place to trot out the last of the Heavy Ten: cultural death. I was going to talk about "cultural burnout"—kind of like how the idealism of the 60s gave way languidly to the hedonism of the 70s, when people couldn't keep up with that amount of morality for very long because it was exhausting. But then I realized sadly that we really don't have a culture. We have a fast-food assembly line of get-rich fads and slim-fast diets, topped off by a healthy dose of new videos on You Tube. People only really get involved when others are watching and only care when they can get money out of you. It's a hellish shame; we used to be so innovative, both spiritually and technically.

In the end, I can't be convinced that I did any good with people when it comes to enlightenment. Some shit is just there for good, like tiny poop pebbles in the fur around a dog's asshole. And who am I to assume I can do anything otherwise? I'm just a guy who sees what is and what could be. At the end of the day, I'm just a singer trying to get people to lighten up and have a good time. The trials of my life have taught me that in order to face the dismal realities of existence, we need to have some levity. It is our national pressure valve, relieving deadly buildup and steeling our resolve for the tribulations of rainy days and bastardizations. If I could, I would take the darkness of all squarely on my shoulders for a while, at least to get us all back home in one piece. Everyone who does their best deserves that respite, if only for the second it takes to catch their breaths and keep going.

So again, let me say that this list—hell, even my new list— should be like the Constitution of the United States: a seemingly living document that is endowed with the bedrock of who we can all be, yet flexible so that it can change and evolve with the times. We are a modern tribe of hunter-gatherers, collecting and killing to survive, resisting the winds and catastrophes that are thrown our way with ever-greater consistency. As we find new ways to live and breathe, we should also find new ways to live in peace. No one should be saddled with more than he or she can handle. There has to be a way to get to tomorrow. So our views of sin cannot be as benign as fighting the concept of contraceptives being approved by health care. They have to be smarter . . . because we are smarter. I believe that. I have to believe that. Our Seven Deadly Sins should be updated for the generations after to understand.

Or if that metaphor doesn't work for you, try this: The Seven Deadly Sins should be updated in the same way the Star Wars movies are constantly tinkered with, though why those movies are touched at all is a fucking mystery to me. At this point, George Lucas is nothing but a god damn drug dealer, because he *knows* we'll keep coming back.

I'll close this special chapter with a tale from the last night of my solo tour, about a little ten-year-old girl named, that's right, Corey Taylor. I'd first met her and her parents at a Stone Sour gig in Florida, where she carried a sign that said "I'm Corey Taylor Too And It's My Birthday!" We pulled her to the side of the stage and let her watch from there, and she had such a good time she walked away one of the happiest kids I'd ever seen.

When she showed up in Tampa for the solo show, she stood protected by her mother in front of the stage, watching and listening, and laughing and singing, even when I made her close her ears before I told the audience an especially offensive story. Afterward she and her mother met us on the bus before we left to go home and her mother told me I was her daughter's hero. I told her she was just tired—it was after all past midnight in the middle of a school week—and she needed to get some sleep. Corey Taylor gave the slightly taller Corey Taylor a big hug, and I sent her and her family home.

But I sat and thought about that for a while. I was a hero to a little girl who wasn't even born by the time I had started my music career. I realized that I could retire right then and I would have no regrets. All I'd wanted to do my whole life was to make a difference, to leave behind evidence that I was here, because as Abraham Lincoln observed that was the only real immortality you could hope for. If everything stopped tomorrow, I'd still be the luckiest guy in the world. I've made a difference to people with my music, and now with my book. That's good enough for me.

So this extra chapter is a way for me to say thank you to everyone who has supported this fucking Midwestern madman for going on thirteen professional years, and to send my love to the people in life who have stuck by me for over twenty years. I know to most people I am the most hated man in the business, a real villain of the music world. Honestly I couldn't care less. Yes, I have seen and done some things that people might misconstrue as the machinations of a certifiable fuckface. But I let that shit roll down my back like rain on a sunny day. I have more people who love me than hate me, and that's good enough for me. Besides, I'd rather nurture those who care than try to coax negative creeps to my side of the field. My devotion to my fans is all-consuming and nonwavering.

In closing, I hope you see both sides of things. It is the only way to view the chaos on an even plain. If I ever impart on you any wisdom, it is these three bits of tawdry yet sturdy advice. One, take your time before answering any supposed wrong. Two, think things through before you make any decision. And finally three, do not be afraid to sacrifice passion for talent. Passion burns itself out quickly, but talent relights the inner flames more than any match.

So from this whore to countless others, I say thank you. Enjoy this extra chapter—I wrote it for you. I'm going to go attempt to cook a meal for my family now without turning my kitchen into a re-creation of Gettysburg. Stay sane, stay (sic), and remember: don't bend over unless you mean it. Good night

ACKNOWLEDGMENTS

I would like to thank the following people for helping me make this dream come true:

Cory Brennan, who put this idea in my head in the first place; Marc Gerald, who helped me narrow down my extreme imagination and focus on a single topic; Ben Schafer and everyone at Perseus for helping me shape and mold this thing into something readable (and for fending off any lawsuits—haha); Paul Brown, who took my ramblings about the art and channeled them into fantastic visuals; Dave, Shawn, Monke, Amber, Jason, Brenna, Jackie, Christine, and everyone else who brought these "sins" to life; Bob Johnsen, Evange Livanos, and everyone at 5B Management for running rampant and helping me deliver; Stubbs and Kirby for pulling the creativity out of me and helping me find the visuals for the photos; and last but not least, my wife Stephanie Taylor, my partner in crime, who always keeps me driven, who went above and beyond to help me get this all together, and who understood just how important this was to me. I couldn't have done this without you, Steph.